"Do give books - religious or otherwise - for Christmas. *They're never fattening, seldom sinful, and permanently personal".*

Lenore Hershey

The Christmas *Songbook*

Wise Publications

London / New York / Paris / Sydney / Copenhagen / Madrid / Tokyo / Berlin

Exclusive Distributors:

Music Sales Limited
8/9 Frith Street, London W1D 3JB, England.

Music Sales Corporation
257 Park Avenue South,
New York, NY 10010,
United States of America

Music Sales Pty Limited
120 Rothschild Avenue, Rosebery,
NSW 2018, Australia.

Order No. AM982487
ISBN 1-8444-9989-8

Compiled & edited by James Sleigh.
Recipes kindly supplied by Mary Sleigh & Linda Lavelle.
Music processed by Barnes Music Engraving.
Designed & art directed by Michael Bell Design.
Illustrated by Arlene Adams.
Front cover 'bow' illustrated by Mark Thomas.
Printed in China.

Poems...

Stories...

Recipes...

Music...

Once *In* Royal *David's* City

Words by **Cecil Alexander** *Music by* **Henry Gauntlett**

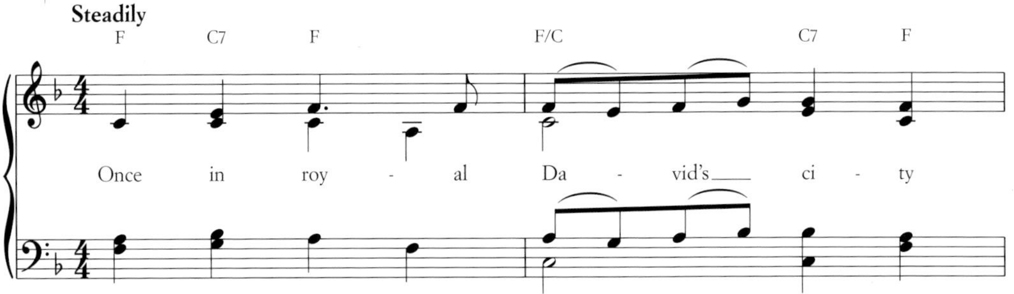

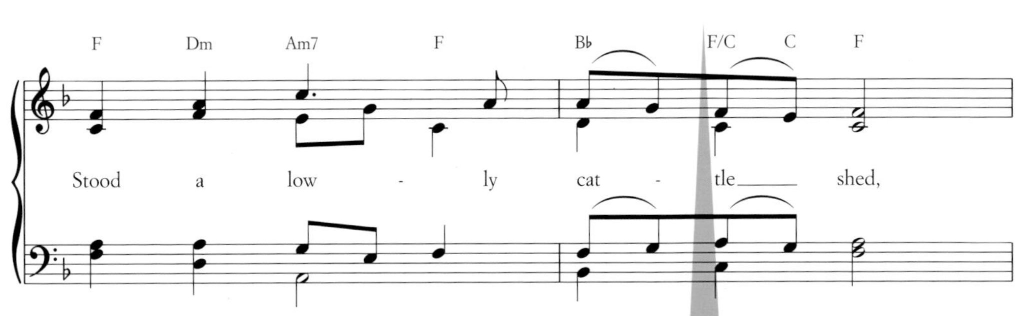

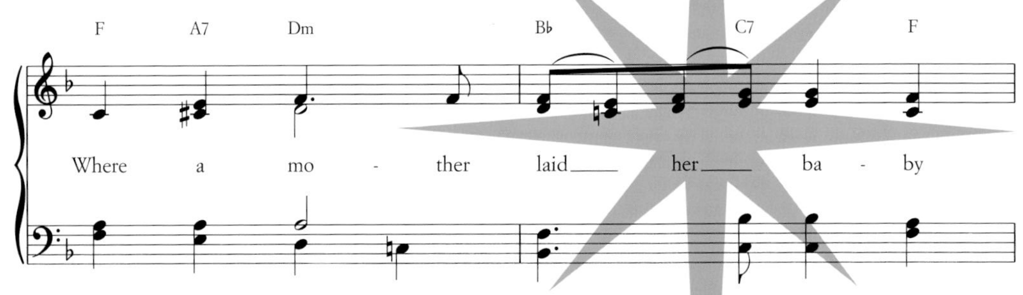

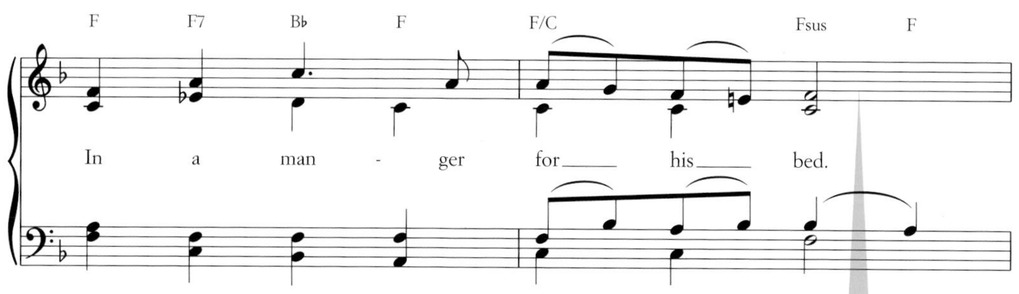

1
Once in royal David's city
Stood a lowly cattle shed,
Where a mother laid her baby
In a manger for his bed.
Mary was that mother mild,
Jesus Christ her little child.

2
He came down to earth from heaven,
Who is God and Lord of all;
And his shelter was a stable,
And his cradle was a stall.
With the poor, and mean, and lowly,
Lived on earth our Saviour holy.

3
And through all his wondrous childhood
He would honour and obey,
Love and watch the lowly maiden,
In whose gentle arms he lay.
Christian children all must be
Mild, obedient, good as he.

4
And our eyes at last shall see him,
Through his own redeeming love,
For that child so dear and gentle
Is our Lord in heaven above;
And he leads his children on
To the place where he is gone.

O *Come* All *Ye* Faithful

Original Words & Music by **John Francis Wade** *English Words by* **Frederick Oakeley**

At a moderate pace
G Am7 D7sus D7 G D G C G/D D Em
O come, all ye faith - ful, Joy - ful and tri - um - phant, O

Em A7 D A7 D E7 D/A A7 D
come ye, O come ye to Beth - le - hem.

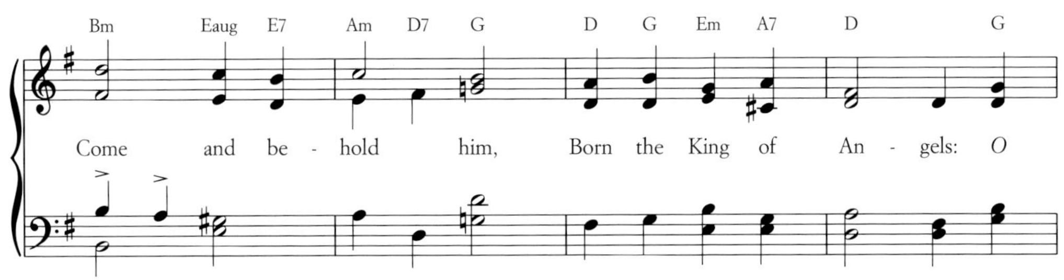

Bm Eaug E7 Am D7 G D G Em A7 D G
Come and be - hold him, Born the King of An - gels: O

1 O come, all ye faithful,
Joyful and triumphant,
O come ye, O come ye to Bethlehem.
Come and behold him,
Born the King of Angels:

O come, let us adore him,
O come, let us adore him,
O come, let us adore him,
Christ the Lord.

2 God of God,
Light of Light,
Lo! he abhors not the Virgin's womb;
Very God,
Begotten, not created:
O come, let us adore him . . .

3 Sing, choirs of angels,
Sing in exultation.
Sing, all ye citizens of heaven above;
Glory to God
In the highest:
O come, let us adore him . . .

4 Yea, Lord, we greet thee,
Born this happy morning,
Jesu, to thee be glory given;
Word of the father,
Now in flesh appearing:
O come, let us adore him . . .

Jingle *Bells*

Words & Music by **J.S. Pierpont**

Moderately, with bounce
G
Gaug
C
Dash - ing through the snow, In a one - horse o - pen sleigh,

C
Am
D7
G
O'er the fields we go, Laugh - ing all the way,

G
G7
C
Bells on Bob - tail ring, Mak - ing spir - its bright, What

C
Am7♭5
G/D
Am7
D7
G
fun it is to ride and sing A sleigh - ing song to - night.

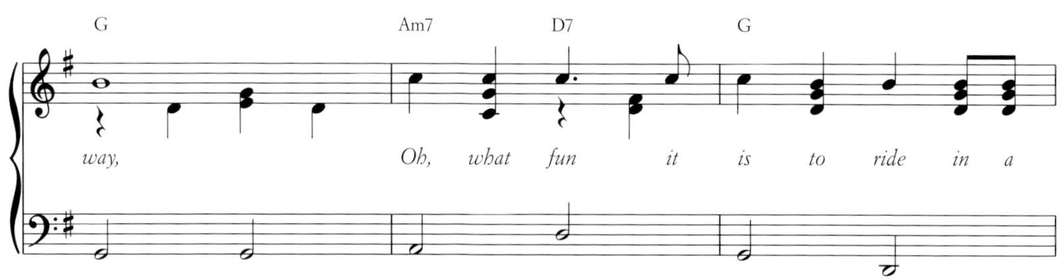

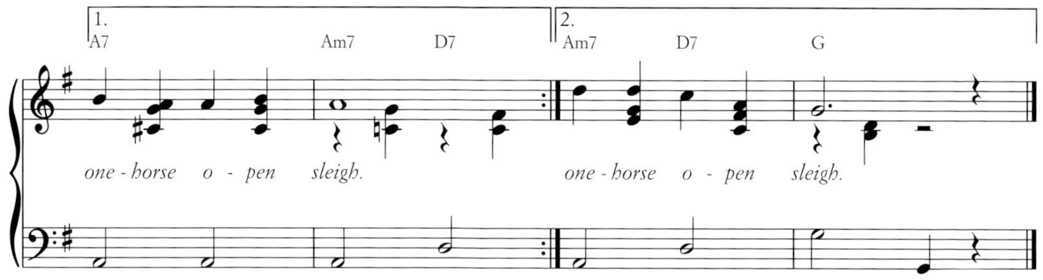

1

Dashing through the snow,
In a one-horse open sleigh,
O'er the fields we go,
Laughing all the way,
Bells on Bobtail ring,
Making spirits bright,
What fun it is to ride and sing
A sleighing song tonight.

Jingle bells, jingle bells,
Jingle all the way,
Oh, what fun it is to ride
In a one-horse open sleigh.

2

A day or two ago
I thought I'd take a ride,
And soon Miss Fannie Bright
Was seated by my side;
The horse was lean and lank,
Misfortune seemed his lot,
He got into a drifted bank,
And then we got upsot!

Jingle bells, jingle bells . . .

The *Holly* And *The* Ivy

Traditional

At a moderate pace

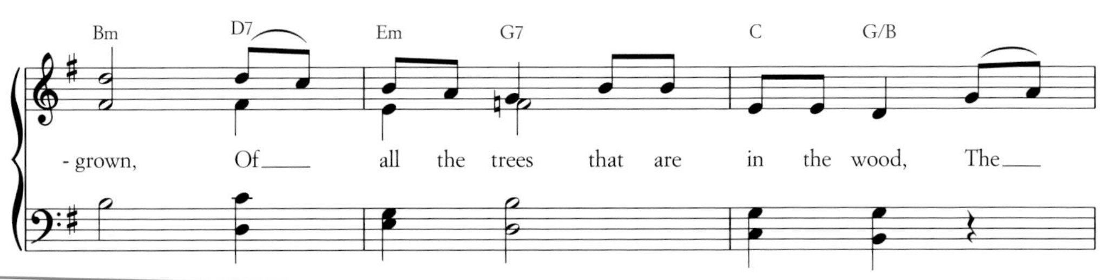

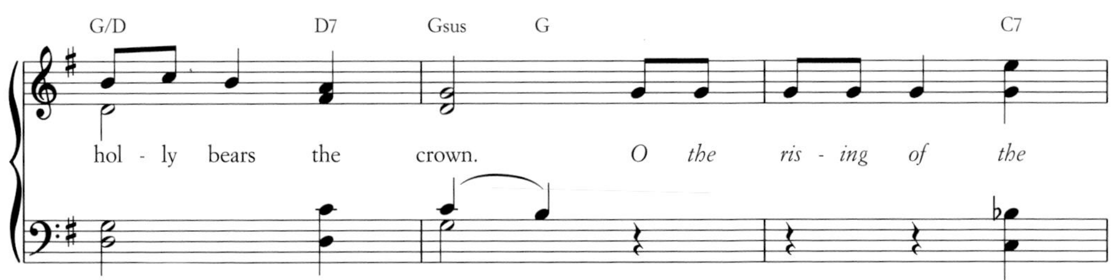

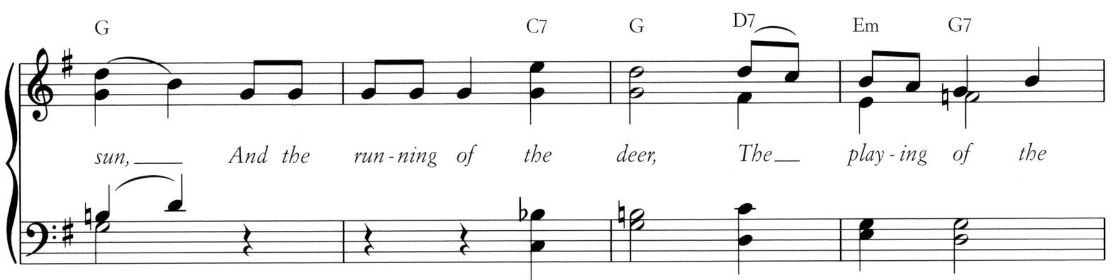

The holly and the ivy,
When they are both full grown,
Of all the trees that are in the wood,
1 The holly bears the crown.

O the rising of the sun,
And the running of the deer,
The playing of the merry organ,
Sweet singing in the choir.

The holly bears the blossom
2 As white as lily flower;
And Mary bore sweet Jesus Christ
To be our sweet Saviour.
O the rising of the sun . . .

The holly bears a berry,
As red as any blood;
3 And Mary bore sweet Jesus Christ
To do poor sinners good.
O the rising of the sun . . .

The holly bears a prickle,
As sharp as any thorn;
4 And Mary bore sweet Jesus Christ
On Christmas Day in the morn.
O the rising of the sun . . .

The holly bears a bark,
As bitter as any gall;
5 And Mary bore sweet Jesus Christ,
For to redeem us all.
O the rising of the sun . . .

O *Christmas* Tree (O Tannenbaum)

Traditional

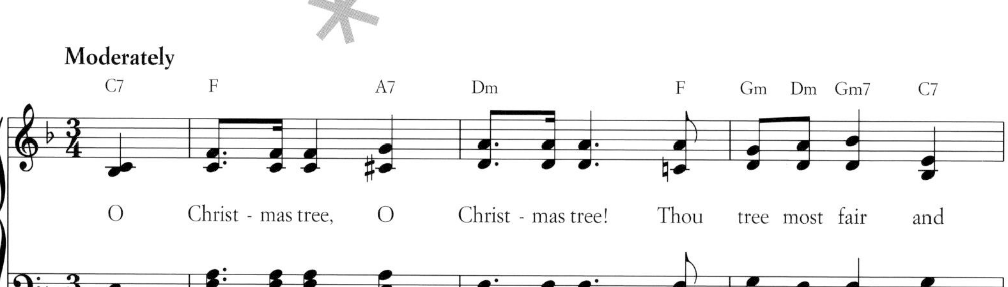
Moderately
C7 F A7 Dm F Gm Dm Gm7 C7
O Christ - mas tree, O Christ - mas tree! Thou tree most fair and

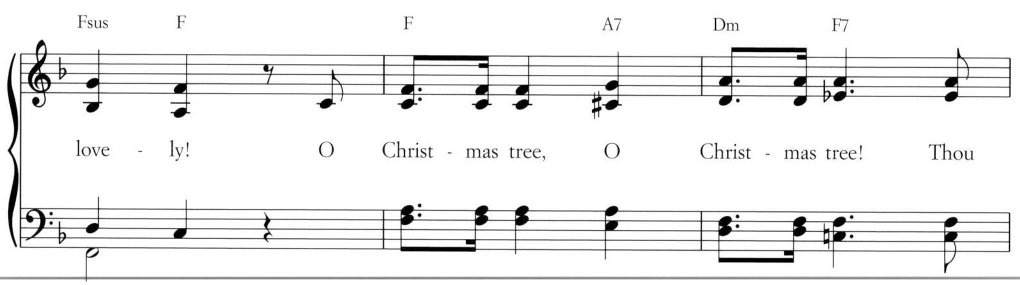
Fsus F F A7 Dm F7
love - ly! O Christ - mas tree, O Christ - mas tree! Thou

Gm Dm Gm7 C7 Fsus4 F F Am7♭5 D7
tree most fair and love - ly! The sight of thee at

© Copyright 2001 Dorsey Brothers Music Limited, 8/9 Frith Street, London W1.
All Rights Reserved. International Copyright Secured.

1 O Christmas tree, O Christmas tree!
Thou tree most fair and lovely!
O Christmas tree, O Christmas tree!
Thou tree most fair and lovely!
The sight of thee at Christmastide
Spreads hope and gladness far and wide,
O Christmas tree, O Christmas tree!
Thou tree most fair and lovely!

2 O Christmas tree, O Christmas tree!
Thou hast a wondrous message.
O Christmas tree, O Christmas tree!
Thou hast a wondrous message.
Thou dost proclaim the Saviour's birth,
Goodwill to men and peace on earth.
O Christmas tree, O Christmas tree!
Thou hast a wondrous message.

The *Cratchits* Celebrate *Christmas* *from* A *Christmas* Carol *by* Charles *Dickens*

Then up rose Mrs. Cratchit, Cratchit's wife, dressed out but poorly in a twice-turned gown, but brave in ribbons, which are cheap and make a goodly show for sixpence; and she laid the cloth, assisted by Belinda Cratchit, second of her daughters, also brave in ribbons; while Master Peter Cratchit plunged a fork into the saucepan of potatoes, and getting the corners of his monstrous shirt collar (Bob's private property, confered upon his son and heir in honour of the day) into his mouth, rejoiced to find himself so gallantly attired, and yearned to show his linen in the fashionable Parks. And now two smaller Cratchits, boy and girl, came tearing in, screaming that outside the baker's they had smelt the goose, and known it for their own; and basking in luxurious thoughts of sage and onion, these young Cratchits danced about the table, and exalted Master Peter Cratchit to the skies, while he (not proud, although his collars nearly choked him) blew the fire, until the slow potatoes bubbling up, knocked loudly at the saucepan lid to be let out and peeled.

'What has ever got your precious father then?' said Mrs. Cratchit. 'And your brother, Tiny Tim! And Martha warn't as late last Christmas Day by half-an-hour!'
'Here's Martha, Mother!' said a girl, appearing as she spoke.

'Here's Martha, Mother!' cried the two young Cratchits. 'Hurrah! There's *such* a goose, Martha!'

'Why, bless your heart alive, my dear, how late you are!' said Mrs. Cratchit, kissing her a dozen times, and taking off her shawl and bonnet for her with officious zeal.

'We'd a deal of work to finish up last night,' replied the girl, 'and had to clear away this morning, Mother!'

'Well! Never mind so long as you are come,' said Mrs Cratchit. 'Sit ye down before the fire, my dear, and have a warm, Lord bless ye!'

'No, no! There's Father coming!' cried the two young Cratchits, who were everywhere at once. 'Hide, Martha, hide!'

So Martha hid herself, and in came little Bob, the father, with at least three feet of

comforter exclusive of the fringe, hanging down before him; and his threadbare clothes darned up and brushed, to look seasonable; and Tiny Tim upon his shoulder. Alas for Tiny Tim, he bore a little crutch, and had his limbs supported by an iron frame!

'Why, where's our Martha?', cried Bob Cratchit, looking around.

'Not coming,' said Mrs Cratchit.

'Not coming!' said Bob, with a sudden declension in his high spirits; for he had been Tim's blood horse all the way from church, and had come home rampant. 'Not coming upon Christmas Day!'

Martha didn't like to see him disappointed, if it were only in joke; so she came out prematurely from behind the closet door, and ran into his arms, while the two young Cratchits hustled Tiny Tim, and bore him off into the wash-house, that he might hear the pudding singing in the copper.

'And how did little Tim behave?' asked Mrs Cratchit, when she rallied Bob on his credulity, and Bob had hugged his daughter to his heart's content.

'As good as gold,' said Bob, 'and better. Somehow he gets thoughtful, sitting by himself so much, and thinks the strangest things you ever heard. He told me, coming home, that he hoped the people saw him in the church, because he was a cripple, and it might be pleasant to them to remember upon Christmas Day, who made lame beggars walk and blind men see.'

Bob's voice was tremulous when he told them this, and trembled more when he said that Tiny Tim was growing strong and hearty.

His active little crutch was heard upon the floor, and back came Tiny Tim before another word was spoken, escorted by his brother and sister to his stool before the fire; and while Bob, turning up his cuffs - as if, poor fellow, they were capable of being made more shabby - compounded some hot mixture in a jug with gin and lemons, and stirred it round and round and put it on the hob to simmer, Master Peter and the two ubiquitous young Cratchits went to fetch the goose, with which the soon returned in high procession.

Such a bustle ensued that you might have thought a goose the rarest of all birds; a feathered phenomenon, to which a black swan was a matter of course, and in truth it was something very like it in that house. Mrs. Cratchit made the gravy (ready beforehand in a little saucepan) hissing hot; Master Peter mashed the potatoes with incredible vigour; Miss Belinda sweetened up the apple sauce; Martha dusted the hot plates; Bob took Tiny Tim beside him in a tiny corner at the table; the two young Cratchits set chairs for everybody, not forgetting themselves, and mounting guard

upon their posts, crammed spoons into their mouths, lest they should shriek for goose before their turn came to be helped. At last the dishes were set on, and grace was said. It was succeeded by a breathless pause, as Mrs Cratchit, looking slowly all along the carving-knife, prepared to plunge it in the breast; but when she did, and when the long-expected gush of stuffing issued forth, one murmur of delight arose all round the board, and even Tiny Tim, excited by the two young Cratchits, beat on the table with the handle of his knife, and feebly cried Hurrah!

There never was such a goose. Bob said he didn't believe there ever was such a goose cooked. Its tenderness and flavour, size and cheapness, were the themes of universal admiration. Eked out by the apple sauce and mashed potatoes, it was a sufficient dinner for the whole family; indeed, as Mrs Cratchit said with great delight (surveying one small atom of a bone upon the dish), they hadn't ate it all at last! Yet everyone had had enough, and the youngest Cratchits, in particular, were steeped in sage and onion to the eyebrows! But now, the plates being changed by Miss Belinda, Mrs Cratchit left the room alone - too nervous to bear witness - to take the pudding up and bring it in.

Suppose it should not be done enough! Suppose it should break in turning out! Suppose somebody should have got over the wall of the back-yard, and stolen it, while they were merry with the goose - a supposition at which the two young Cratchits became livid! All sorts of horrors were supposed.

Halloa! A great deal of steam! The pudding was out of the copper. A smell like a washing-day! That was the cloth. A smell like an eating-house and a pastry-cook's next door to each other, with a laundress's next door to that! That was the pudding! In half a minute Mrs Cratchit entered - flushed, but smiling proudly - with the pudding, like a speckled cannonball, so hard and firm, blazing in half of half a quartern of ignited brandy, and bedight with Christmas holly stuck into the top.

Oh, a wondeful pudding! Bob Cratchit said, and calmly too, that he regarded it as the greatest success achieved by Mrs Cratchit since their marriage. Mrs Cratchit said that now the weight was off her mind, she would confess she had had her doubts about the quantity of flour. Everybody had something to say about it, but nobody said or thought it was at all a small pudding for a large family. It would have been flat heresy to do so. Any Cratchit would have blushed to hint at such a thing.

At last the dinner was all done, the cloth was cleared, the hearth swept, and the fire made up. The compound in the jug being tasted, and considered perfect, apples and oranges were put upon the table, and a shovelful of chestnuts upon the fire. Then all the

Cratchit family drew round the hearth in what Bob Cratchit called a circle, meaning half a one; and at Bob Cratchit's elbow stood the family display of glass. Two tumblers, and a custard-cup without a handle.

These held the hot stuff from the jug, however, as well as golden goblets would have done; and Bob served it out with beaming looks, while the chestnuts on the fire sputtered and cracked noisily. Then Bob proposed:

'A Merry Christmas to us all, my dears. God bless us!'

Which all the family re-echoed.

'God bless us everyone!' said Tiny Tim, the last of all.

Winter

Lord Tennyson (1809-92)

The frost is here,
The fuel is dear
And woods are sear,
And fires burn clear,
And frost is here
And has bitten the heel of the going year.

Bite, frost, bite!
You roll up away from the light,
The blue-wood-louse and the plump dormouse,
And the bees are stilled and the fires are killed,
And you bite far into the heart of the house,
But not into mine.

Bite, frost, bite!
The woods are all the searer,
The fuel is all the dearer,
The fires are all the clearer,
My spring is all the nearer,
You have bitten into the heart of the earth,
But not into mine

While *Shepherds* Watched

Music: **Traditional** *Words by* **Nahum Tate**

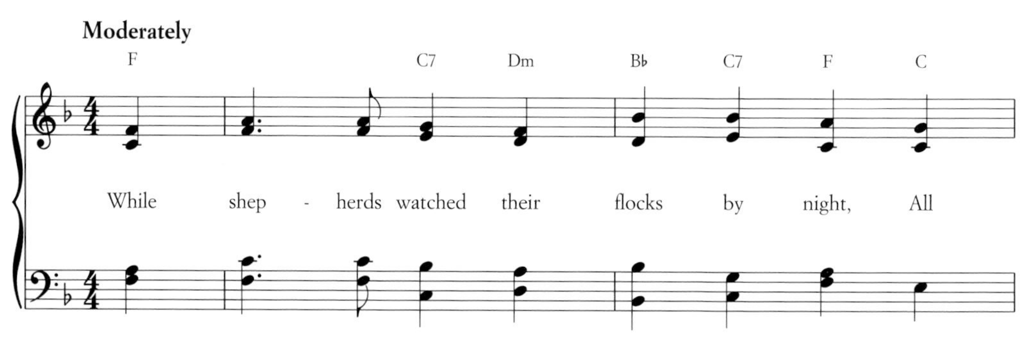
Moderately
F C7 Dm Bb C7 F C
While shep - herds watched their flocks by night, All

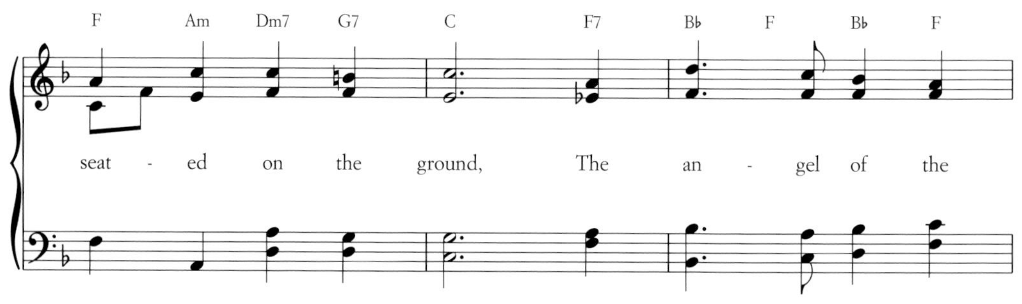
F Am Dm7 G7 C F7 Bb F Bb F
seat - ed on the ground, The an - gel of the

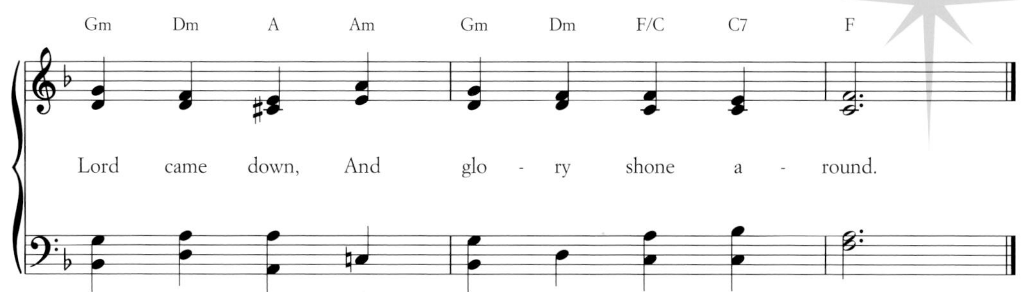

1 While shepherds watched their flocks by night,
All seated on the ground,
The angel of the Lord came down,
And glory shone around.

2 'Fear not,' said he; for mighty dread
Had seized their troubled mind;
'Glad tidings of great joy I bring
To you and all mankind.'

3 'To you in David's town this day
Is born of David's line
A Saviour, who is Christ the Lord;
And this shall be the sign:'

4 'The heavenly Babe you there shall find
To human view displayed,
All meanly wrapped in swaddling bands,
And in a manger laid.'

5 Thus spake the seraph; and forthwith
Appeared a shining throng
Of angels praising God, who thus
Addressed their joyful song:

6 'All glory be to God on high,
And to the earth be peace;
Goodwill henceforth from heaven to men
Begin and never cease!'

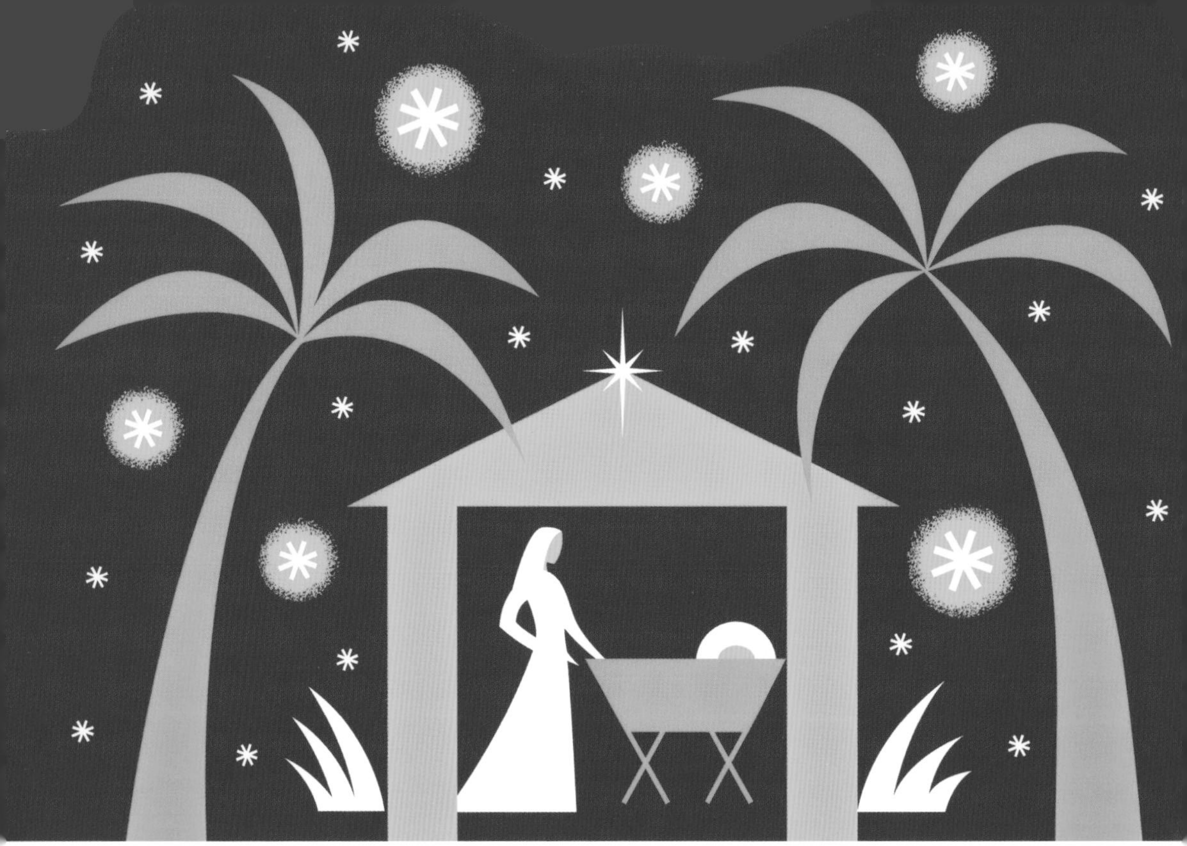

Away *In A Manger*

Words: **Traditional** *Music by* **William Kirkpatrick**

1 Away in a manger, no crib for a bed,
The little Lord Jesus laid down his sweet head.
The stars in the bright sky looked down where he lay,
The little Lord Jesus asleep on the hay.

2 The cattle are lowing, the baby awakes,
But little Lord Jesus, no crying he makes.
I love thee, Lord Jesus! Look down from the sky,
And stay by my side until morning is nigh.

3 Be near me Lord Jesus; I ask thee to stay
Close by me for ever, and love me, I pray.
Bless all the dear children in they tender care,
And fit us for heaven, to live with thee there.

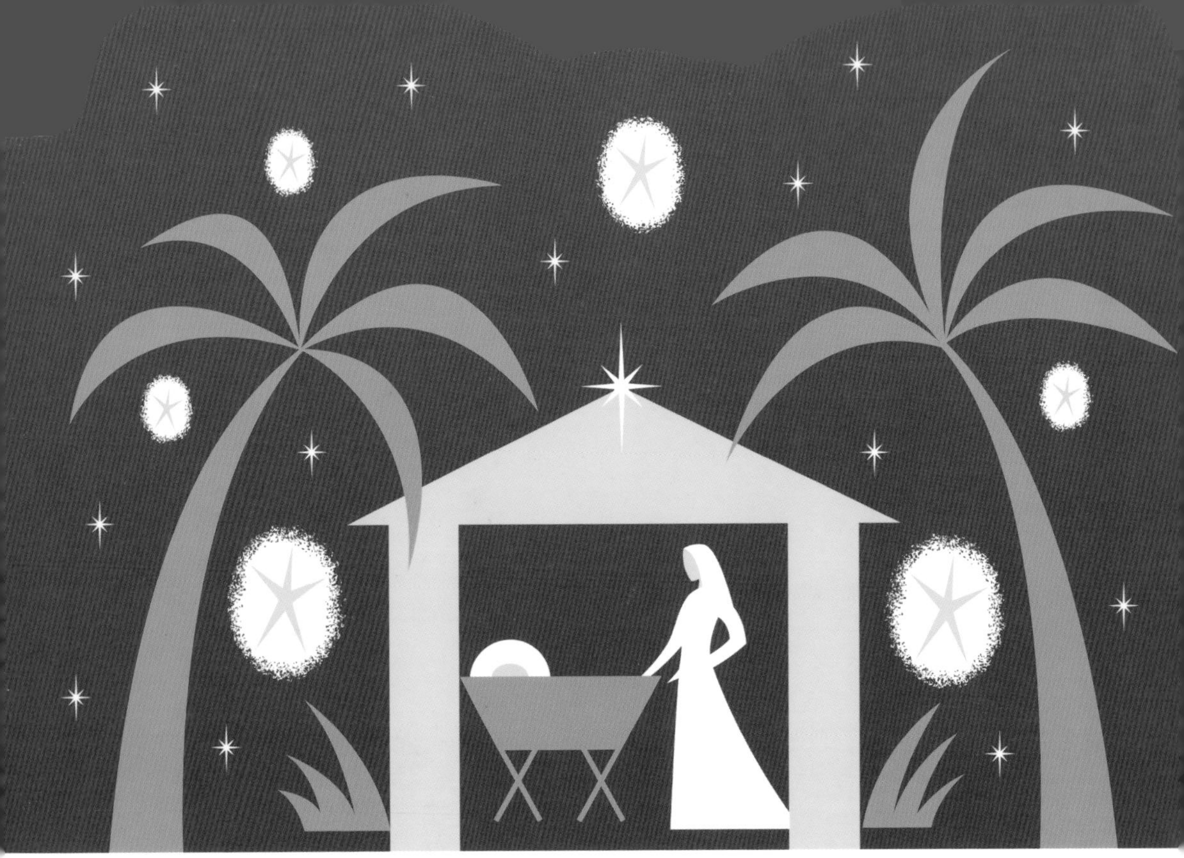

Away *In A Manger*

U.S. Tune Words: **Traditional** *Music by* ***James R. Murray (1841-1905)***

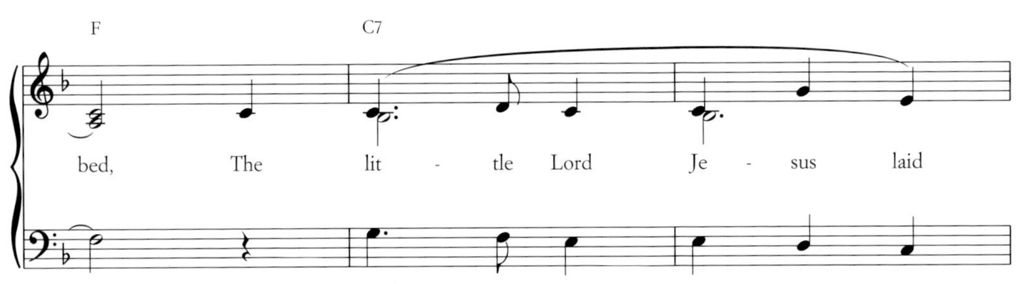

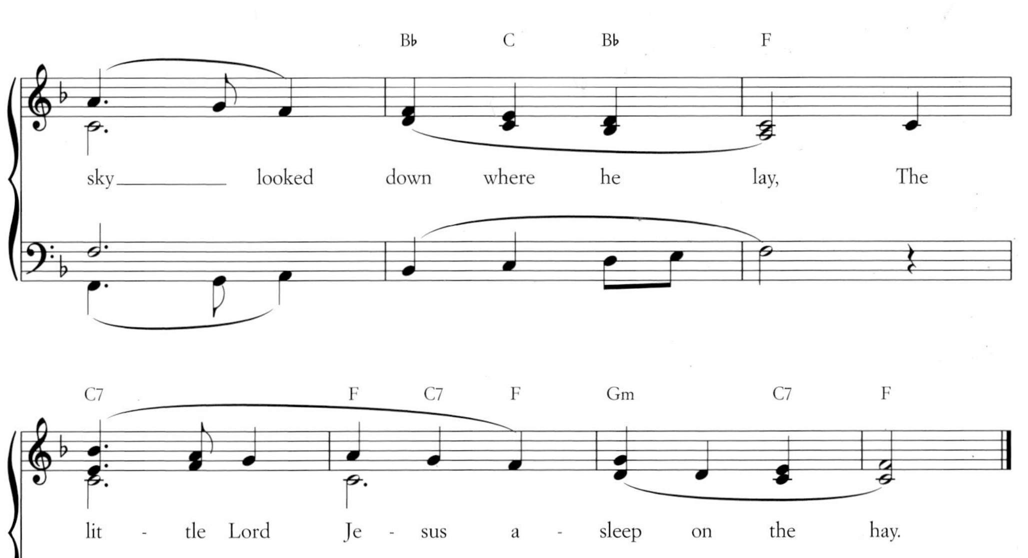

1 Away in a manger, no crib for a bed,
The little Lord Jesus laid down his sweet head.
The stars in the sky looked down where he lay,
The little Lord Jesus asleep on the hay.

2 The cattle are lowing, the baby awakes,
But little Lord Jesus, no crying he makes.
I love thee, Lord Jesus! Look down from the sky,
And stay by my side until morning is nigh.

3 Be near me Lord Jesus; I ask thee to stay
Close by me for ever, and love me, I pray.
Bless all the dear children in thy tender care,
And fit us for heaven, to live with thee there.

The *First* Nowell

Traditional

Brightly

A7 D A7 D A7 D/F♯ G D A7

The first No - well the an - gel did say Was to

D/F♯ G D/F♯ G A7 D/F♯ D/A A7 D A7

cer - tain poor shep - herds in fields as they lay; In

D A7 D A7 D/F♯ G D A7

fields where they lay keep - ing their sheep, On a

D/F♯ G D/F♯ G A7 Bm Em7 A7 D F♯7

cold win - ter's night that was so deep: *No -*

Bm A7 D/F♯ G C♯7 F♯m A7 D

- well, No - well, No - well, No - well,

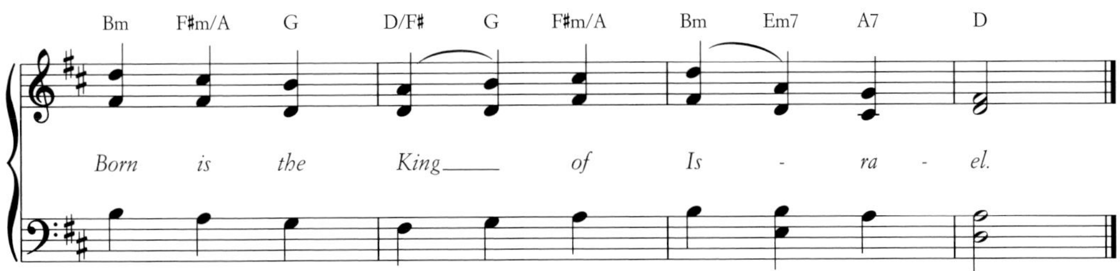
Bm F#m/A G D/F# G F#m/A Bm Em7 A7 D
Born is the King of Is - ra - el.

1 The first Nowell the angel did say
Was to certain poor shepherds in fields as they lay;
In fields where they lay keeping their sheep,
On a cold winter's night that was so deep:

Nowell, Nowell, Nowell, Nowell,
Born is the King of Israel.

2 They lookèd up and saw a star
Shining in the east, beyond them far;
And to the earth it gave great light,
And so it continued both day and night:
Nowell, Nowell . . .

3 And by the light of that same star,
Three Wise Men came from country far;
To seek for a king was their intent,
And to follow the star wherever it went:
Nowell, Nowell . . .

4 This star drew nigh unto the north-west;
O'er Bethlehem it took its rest,
And there it did both stop and stay,
Right over the place where Jesus lay:
Nowell, Nowell . . .

5* Then did they know assuredly
Within that house the King did lie:
One entered in then for to see,
And found the babe in poverty:
Nowell, Nowell . . .

6 Then entered in those Wise Men three,
Fell reverently upon their knee,
And offered there, in his presence,
Their gold and myrrh and frankincense:
Nowell, Nowell . . .

7* Between an ox-stall and an ass
This child truly there born he was;
For want of clothing they did him lay
All in a manger, among the hay:
Nowell, Nowell . . .

8 Then let us all with one accord
Sing praises to our heavenly Lord,
That hath made heaven and earth of naught,
And with his blood mankind hath bought:
Nowell, Nowell . . .

9* If we in our time shall do well,
We shall be free from death and hell;
For God hath preparèd for us all
A resting place in general:
Nowell, Nowell . . .

* Verses usually omitted.

O *Come,* O *Come,* Emmanuel

Traditional *English Words by* ***John Neale***

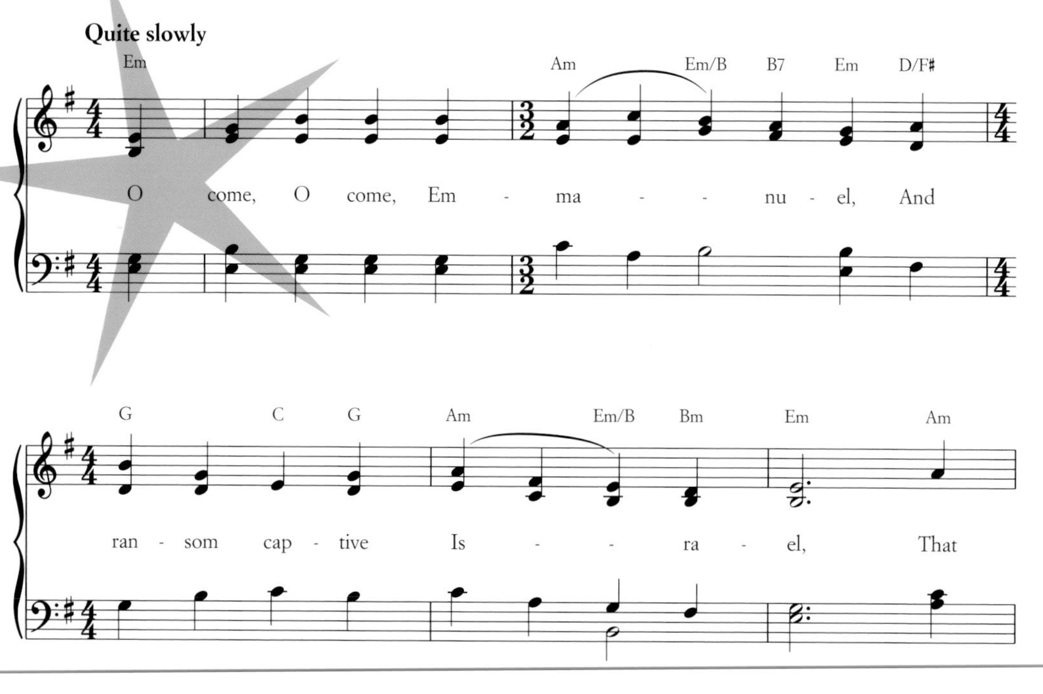

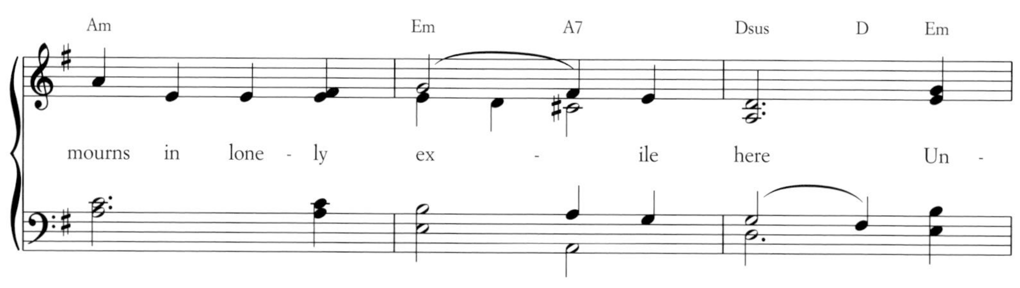

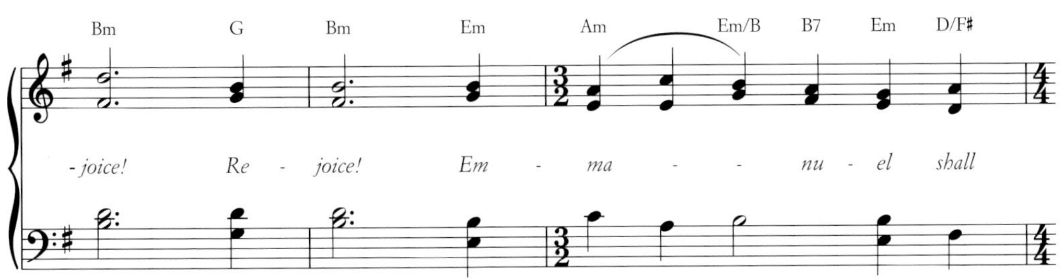

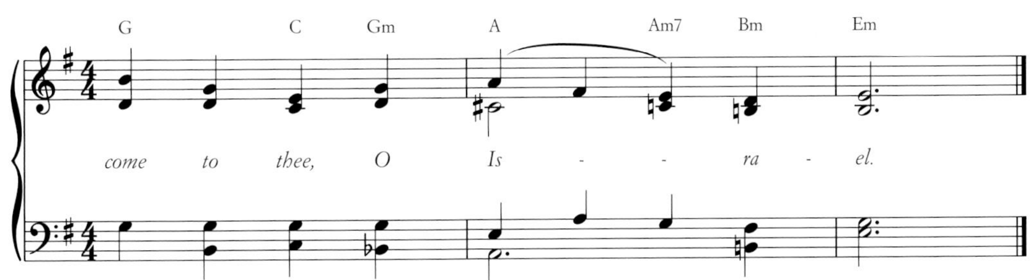

1 O come, O come, Emmanuel,
And ransom captive Israel,
That mourns in lonely exile here
Until the Son of God appear.

Rejoice! Rejoice!
Emmanuel shall come to thee, O Israel.

2 O come, thou rod of Jesse, free
Thine own from Satan's tyranny;
From depths of hell thy people save,
And give them victory o'er the grave.
Rejoice! . . .

3 O come, thou dayspring, come and cheer
Our spirits by thine advent here;
Disperse the gloomy clouds of night,
And death's dark shadows put to flight.
Rejoice! . . .

4 O come, o come, thou Lord of might,
Who to thy tribes, on Sinai's height,
In ancient times didst give the law
In cloud, and majesty and awe.
Rejoice! . . .

5 O come, thou key of David, come,
And span wide our heavenly home;
Make safe the way that leads on high,
And close the path to misery.
Rejoice! . . .

We *Three* Kings Of Orient *Are*

Words & Music by **John Henry Hopkins**

Smooth and flowing

Em Am Em Am Em Em Am Em Am Em

We three Kings of O - ri - ent are; Bear - ing gifts we tra-verse a - far,

Em Am7♭5 G/D D7 Bm Am Em/B B7

Field and foun - tain, moor and moun - tain, Fol - low - ing yon - der

Em D G C G

star: *O______ star of won - der, star of night,*

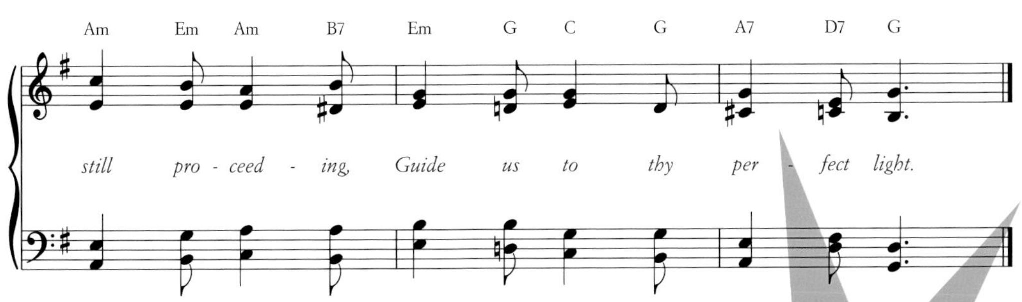

1 We three Kings of Orient are;
Bearing gifts we traverse afar,
Field and fountain, moor and mountain,
Following yonder star:

O star of wonder, star of night,
Star with royal beauty bright,
Westward leading, still proceeding,
Guide us to thy perfect light.

2 Born a King on Bethlehem plain,
Gold I bring, to crown him again,
King for ever, ceasing never,
Over us all to reign:
O star of wonder, star of night . . .

3 Frankincense to offer have I,
Incense owns a Deity nigh;
Prayer and praising, all men raising,
Worship him, God most high:
O star of wonder, star of night . . .

4 Myrrh is mine, its bitter perfume
Breathes a life of gathering gloom;
Sorrowing, sighing, bleeding, dying,
Sealed in the stone-cold tomb:
O star of wonder, star of night . . .

5 Glorious now, behold him arise,
King and God and sacrifice!
Heaven sings alleluia
Alleluia the earth replies:
O star of wonder, star of night . . .

The *Castle* Of *Ice* from *The* Snow *Queen* by *Hans* Christian *Andersen*

They stopped at a small house. It was a miserable place, whose roof came almost down to the ground, and whose door was so low that the family had to crawl on their stomachs whenever they wanted to go in or out. Except for an old Lapp woman, who was cooking fish over an oil stove, there was nobody in the house. The reindeer told her Gerda's story, but first of all he told his own, which seemed to him to be much more important. And Gerda was so pinched with the cold that she couldn't speak.

'Oh! you poor dears!' said the Lapp woman. 'You've still got a long way to go. You must travel hundreds of miles into Finnmark, for it's there that the Snow Queen lives in the country and burns Bengal lights every evening. I'll write a few words on a dry cod – I haven't any paper – and give them to you for the Finn woman who lives up there. She can tell can you more than I can.'

When Gerda had got warm again and had had something to eat and drink, the Lapp woman wrote a few words on a dried cod, told Gerda to take great care of it, and tied her firmly on the reindeer's back again, and off they went. Whizz! bang! up in the air the most beautiful blue Northern Lights glowed all night long. At last they reached Finnmark and knocked at the Finn woman's chimney, for she hadn't even got a door!

Inside it was so hot that the Finn woman herself went about almost naked. She was small and dirty. She immediately undid little Gerda's clothes and pulled off her mittens and her shoes, otherwise she'd have been too hot. Then she put a piece of ice on the reindeer's head and read what was written on the cod. She read it three times, and then she knew it by heart, so she popped the fish into the cooking pot, for it might just as well be eaten, and she never wasted anything.

Then the reindeer told first his own story and then little Gerda's. The Finn woman blinked her wise eyes, but said nothing.

'You are very wise,' said the reindeer. 'I know that you can bind all the winds together with one piece of cotton. When the pilot undoes the first knot, he gets a fair

wind; when he undoes the second, it begins to blow hard; and when he undoes the third and the fourth knots, then comes a tempest that blows down the forests! Won't you prepare a potion for the little girl that will give her the strength of twelve men, and so let her overcome the Snow Queen?'

'The strength of twelve men?' said the Finn woman. 'That would be worth having, certainly.'

She went over to a shelf and took from it a large rolled-up pelt and opened it. On it strange letters were written, and the Finn woman read it until the perspiration poured down from her forehead.

But the reindeer begged so hard on little Gerda's behalf, and Gerda looked at the Finn woman with such beseeching eyes, full of tears, that she began once more to blink her own eyes; then she drew the reindeer into a corner, where they whispered together, and she put some more ice on his head.

'Little Kay is with the Snow Queen sure enough and he is finding everything there very much to his liking, and thinks it the best place in the world. But that's because he has a splinter of glass in his heart and a grain of glass in his eye. They must be got out first of all; otherwise he'll never become a human being again, and the Snow Queen will retain her power over him.'

'But can't you give Gerda something that will give her power over everything?'

'I can give her no greater power than that which she now possesses. Don't you see how great it is? Don't you see how men and beasts are compelled to serve her, and how wonderfully she has covered the wide world on her bare feet? She cannot get her power from us; it's there, in her heart, just because she is a sweet and innocent child. If she can't herself make her way to the Snow Queen and get the bits of glass out of Kay, then we cannot help her. Two miles from here the Snow Queen's garden begins. You can carry the little girl as far as that, and put her down beside a bush with red berries standing in the snow. Don't stop and chatter, but hurry straight back here.' The Finn woman then lifted Gerda on to the reindeer, who ran off as fast as he could.

'Oh! I haven't got my boots! I haven't got my mittens!' cried little Gerda. In the bitter cold she noticed it at once. But the reindeer dared not stop; he ran on until they reached the bush with the red berries. There he set Gerda down and kissed her on the mouth. Great big tears rolled down the animal's cheeks, and then he ran back as fast as he could go. And there stood poor Gerda, without shoes and without gloves in the middle of the terrible, ice-cold Finnmark.

She ran forward as fast as she could. Towards her came a whole regiment of snowflakes; but they were not falling from the sky, which was quite clear and bright with the Northern Lights. The snowflakes ran along the ground, and the nearer they came, the bigger they grew. Gerda remembered how big and wonderfully made the snowflakes had looked that time when she had seen them through the magnifying glass. But these here were certainly much bigger and much more frightening. They were alive; they were the Snow Queen's guards, and they had strange shapes. Some of them looked like great ugly hedgehogs; others like a bunches of knotted snakes, sticking their heads out; and others again were like small, fat bears, whose hair stood on end. All were dazzling white, and all were living snowflakes.

Little Gerda said the Lord's prayer. And the cold was so great that she could see her own breath coming out of her mouth like smoke. It grew thicker and thicker and formed itself into little Angels, who grew bigger and bigger as soon as they reached the ground. All had helmets on their heads and spears and shields in their hands. Their numbers became greater and greater, and by the time Gerda had finished the Lord's prayer, there was a whole legion of them. They charged with their spears against the hateful snowflakes, so that they were splintered into a hundred pieces; and little Gerda went forward confidently and with a stout heart. The Angels stroked her hands and feet, and immediately she felt the cold less and hastened on to the Snow Queen's castle.

But now, before we go any further, we must see what Kay was doing. He certainly wasn't thinking about little Gerda, and least of all that she was standing there outside the castle.

The walls of the castle were built of the driven snow, and the windows and doors of the cutting wind. There were more than a hundred halls, all just as the snow had formed them. The biggest of them was many miles long, and the strong north light illumined them all, however vast and empty, and however cold and glittering they were. Here there was never any fun, not even a dancing bear, though the storm might have played for it and polar bears might have stood on their hind legs and done their pretty tricks; never a little party to play Slap-mouth or Pat-paw; never even a coffee party for the white lady foxes. Empty, big and cold were the halls of the Snow Queen's castle. The Northern Lights shone so steadily that you could tell exactly when they were at their highest and when at their lowest. In the midst of these unending empty halls of snow was a frozen lake, broken into a thousand pieces. But each piece was exactly like the others, and the whole was a perfect work of art. And in the middle of the lake sat

the Snow Queen, when she was home, and then she used to say that she sat in the in Mirror of Wisdom and that it was the only one, and the best in the world.

Little Kay was blue with cold indeed, almost black; but he didn't notice it, for she had kissed away the shudders of cold from him, and his heart was like a lump of ice. He was pushing a number of sharp-edged, flat pieces of ice about, pushing and pulling them this way and that, as if he were trying to make something, just as you may have a lot of little pieces of wood and try to make patterns with them in what is called a Chinese Puzzle. Kay went on making patterns, and some of them were truly wonderful. That was the Intellectual Ice Game. In his eyes the patterns were absolutely marvellous and of the greatest importance. That was because of the grain of glass in his eye. He made perfect patterns which formed written words; but he never succeeded in laying the bits to make the word he wanted, the word Eternity. The Snow Queen had said: 'If you can find out that pattern, then you shall be your own master, and I will give you the whole world and a new pair of skates.' But he couldn't do it.

'Now I shall fly away to the warm lands,' said the Snow Queen. 'I will go there and look into the black pots!' (That was what they called the fire-spitting mountains, Etna and Vesuvius). 'I'll make them a little white! That's as it should be! It's good for the lemons and vines.' And the Snow Queen flew away, and Kay sat all alone in the great empty Ice Halls, mile upon mile of them, and gazed at the ice fragments and thought and thought until he crackled. Stiff and quiet he sat there; you'd have thought he was frozen.

Just at that moment little Gerda stepped through the great gate into the castle. A cutting wind was howling, but she said an evening prayer and the winds died down as if they meant to go to sleep; and she stepped into the big empty cold halls. Then she saw Kay, recognised him, and flew to him and put her arms round his neck. She held him fast and cried: 'Kay! darling little Kay! At last I have found you!'

But he sat quite still and stiff and cold. Then little Gerda wept hot tears, which fell on to his breast. They sank into his heart and melted the lump of ice that was there and destroyed the splinter of glass. Kay looked at her and she sang:

'Where roses grow in the hedgerows wild,
There we meet the Holy Child.'

Then Kay started to weep. He wept so hard that the grain of glass swam out of his eye, and then he recognised her and cried joyfully: 'Gerda! Darling little Gerda! Where have

you been for so long? And where have I been?' And he looked round. 'How cold it is here! How big and empty!" And he held fast to Gerda, and she laughed and cried for joy. It was all so wonderful that the very ice chips danced round for joy, and when they got tired and sat down, they arranged themselves exactly so as to make those letters, which the Snow Queen had said that if he could find, then he would be his own master, and she would give him the whole world and a new pair of skates.

Gerda kissed his cheeks and they began to glow; she kissed his eyes, and they shone like her own; she kissed his hands and feet, and he became healthy and full of spirit. The Snow Queen could come home now! His release stood there, written in letters of glittering ice!

They took each other by the hand and wandered out of the great castle. They talked about their grandmother and the roses on the roof. And wherever they went, the wind was stilled and the sun shone. When they came to the bush with the red berries, there stood the reindeer waiting for them. He had brought another young reindeer with him; her udders were full, and she gave the children warm milk and kissed them on the mouth.

Then they carried Kay and Gerda first to the Finn woman, where they got nice and warm in the hot room and were told exactly how to get home, and then to the Lapp woman, who had made new clothes for them and put their sledge in good order.

The reindeer and the young doe ran along beside them and accompanied them to the boundary of the land, where the first green things were sprouting. There they took leave of the Lapp woman and the reindeers. 'Goodbye!' cried everybody. And the first little birds began to twitter and there were green buds in the woods, out of which, mounted on a magnificent horse (Gerda recognised it – it had been harnessed to the golden coach) there rode a young maiden with a splendid red cap on her head, and pistols in her holsters. It was the little robber maid, who was tired of staying at home and was now setting out towards the North, or later, if that didn't suit her, to some other part of the world. She recognised Gerda at once, and Gerda recognised her, and there was great joy. 'You're a fine sort of a fellow to go careering all over the world after!' said the robber maid to little Kay. 'I wonder if you're worth it!'

But Gerda patted her cheeks and asked about the Prince and Princess.

'They have gone abroad,' said the robber maid.

'And the crow?' asked Gerda.

'Oh! the crow is dead,' she replied. 'The tame sweetheart has become a widow and goes about with a little piece of black cloth round her leg. She complains bitterly; but

that's all my eye! But now tell how you got on and how you managed to get him away.'

And Gerda and Kay told her.

'Snip-snap-slipperty-slap!' said the robber maid, shook them both by the hand and promised that if she ever came to their town, she would come and see them. And then off she rode into the wide world.

Gerda and Kay went on hand in hand, and as they went along it was beautifully spring all round them, with flowers and green foliage. The church bells rang, and they recognised the high towers and the town – it was the very town in which they lived. They entered it and went straight to their grandmother's door, up the stairs and into the room, where everything was just as it had been before. The clock was going tick! tock! and the hands moved round. But as they went through the door they saw that they had become grown-up people. The roses on the roof turned their blossoms towards the open window, and there still stood the little children's stools. And Gerda and Kay went and sat down, each on their own and held hands. The cold, empty magnificence in the Snow Queen's castle they had forgotten like a bad dream. Their grandmother sat in God's sunshine and read aloud from the Bible: 'Except ye become as little children, ye shall in on wise enter the Kingdom of Heaven.' And Kay and Gerda gazed into each other's eyes, and suddenly they understood the meaning of the old hymn:

'Where roses grow in the hedgerows wild,
There we meet the Holy Child.'

There they both sat, grown-up yet still children, children in their hearts; and it was summer – warm, kindly summer.

Long, Long Ago
Anon

Winds through the olive trees
Softly did blow
Round little Bethlehem
Long, long ago.

Sheep on the hillside lay
Whiter than snow
Shepherds were watching them
Long, long ago.

Then from the happy sky,
Angels bent low
Singing their songs of joy,
Long, long ago.

For in a manger bed,
Cradled we know
Christ came to Bethlehem
Long, long ago.

See *Amid* The *Winter's* Snow

Words by **Edward Caswall** *Music by* ***John Goss***

Gently, not fast

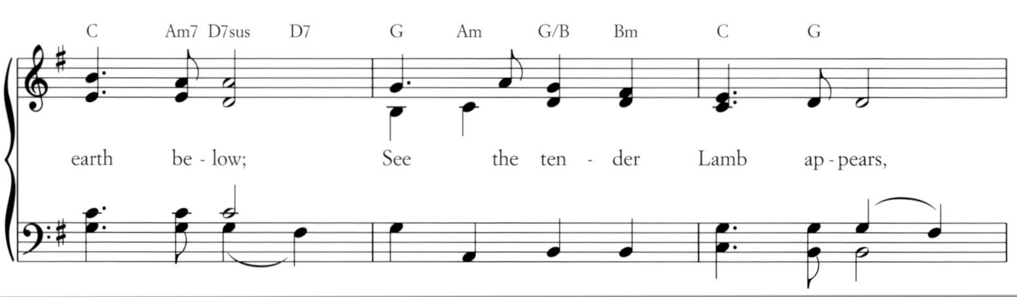

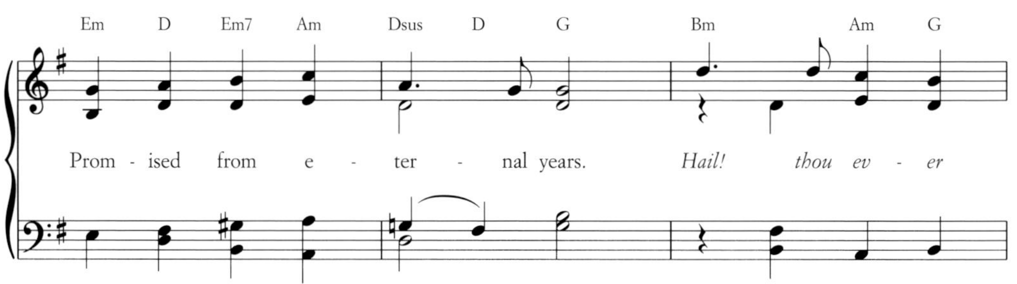

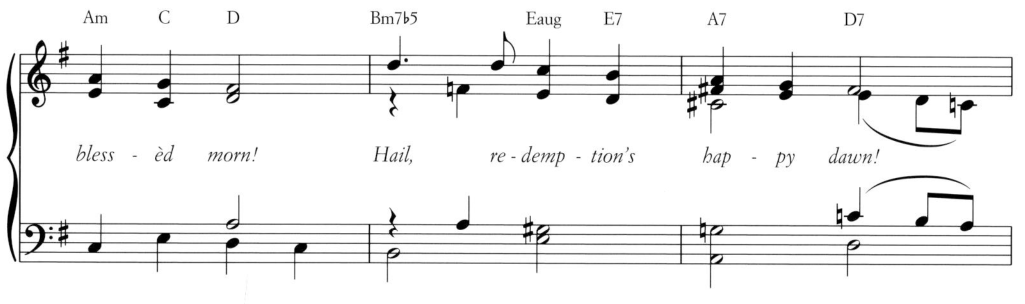

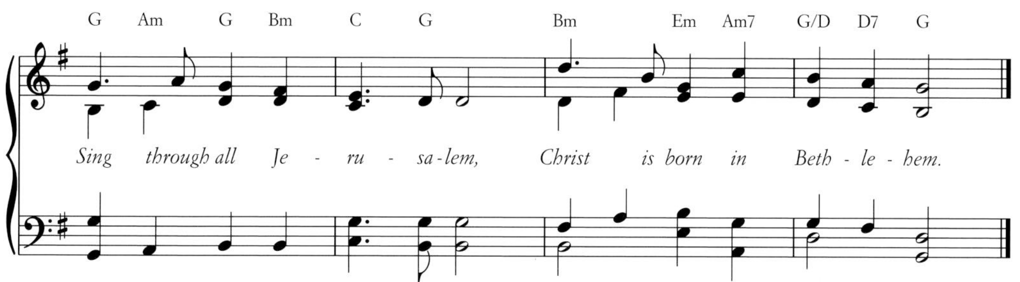

1 See amid the winter's snow,
Born for us on earth below;
See the tender Lamb appears,
Promised from eternal years.

Hail! thou ever blessèd morn!
Hail, redemption's happy dawn!
Sing through all Jerusalem,
Christ is born in Bethlehem.

2 Lo, within a manger lies,
He who built the starry skies;
He who, throned in height sublime,
Sits amid the cherubim.
Hail! thou ever blessèd morn . . .

3 Say, ye holy shepherds, say,
What your joyful news today;
Wherefore have ye left your sheep
On the lonely mountain steep?
Hail! thou ever blessèd morn . . .

4 'As we watched at dead of night,
Lo, we saw a wondrous light;
Angels singing 'Peace on earth',
Told us of the Saviour's birth.'
Hail! thou ever blessèd morn . . .

5 Sacred Infant, all divine,
What a tender love was thine;
Thus to come from highest bliss
Down to such a world as this!
Hail! thou ever blessèd morn . . .

6 Teach, O teach us, Holy Child,
By thy face so meek and mild;
Teach us to resemble thee
In thy sweet humility.
Hail! thou ever blessèd morn . . .

Good *Christian* Men *Rejoice*

Music: **Traditional** *Words by* ***John Neale***

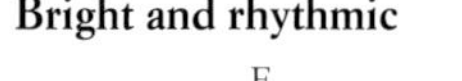
Bright and rhythmic

F
C
Dm
Good Christ - ian men, re - joice! With heart and soul and

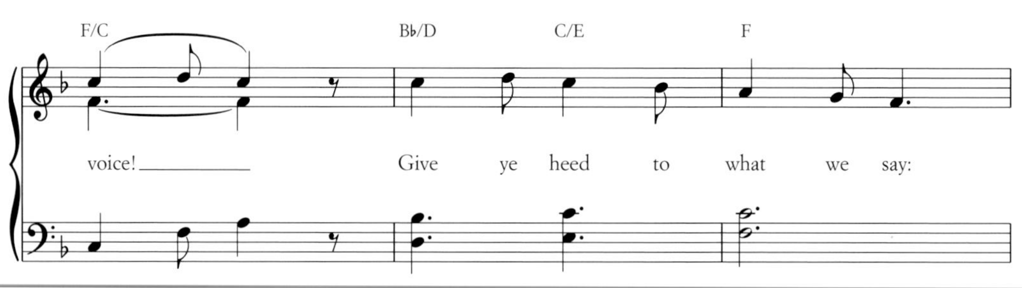
F/C
B♭/D
C/E
F
voice! Give ye heed to what we say:

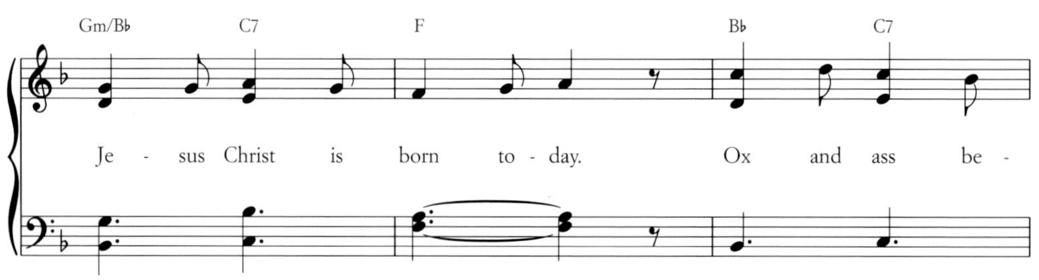
Gm/B♭
C7
F
B♭
C7
Je - sus Christ is born to - day. Ox and ass be -

© Copyright 2001 Dorsey Brothers Music Limited, 8/9 Frith Street, London W1.
All Rights Reserved. International Copyright Secured.

1
Good Christian men, rejoice!
With heart and soul and voice!
Give ye heed to what we say:
Jesus Christ is born today.
Ox and ass before him bow,
And he is in the manger now:
Christ is born today,
Christ is born today.

2
Good Christian men, rejoice!
With heart and soul and voice!
Now ye hear of endless bliss:
Jesus Christ was born for this.
He hath oped the heavenly door,
And man is blessed for ever more:
Christ was born for this,
Christ was born for this.

3
Good Christian men, rejoice!
With heart and soul and voice!
Now ye need not fear the grave:
Jesus Christ was born to save;
Calls you one, and calls you all,
To gain his everlasting hall:
Christ was born to save,
Christ was born to save.

We *Wish* You *A* Merry *Christmas*

Traditional

Brightly

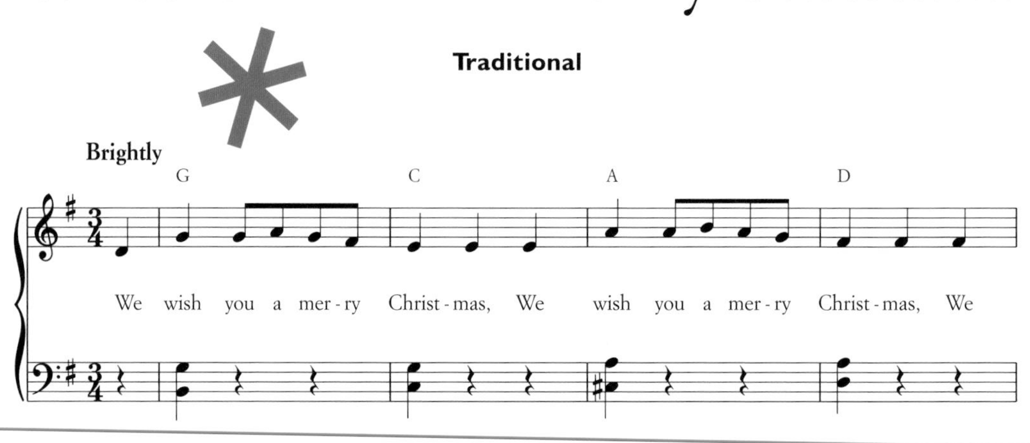

1
We wish you a merry Christmas,
We wish you a merry Christmas,
We wish you a merry Christmas
And a happy New Year.

Good tidings we bring
To you and your kin;
We wish you a merry Christmas
And a happy New Year.

2
We all want some figgy pudding,
We all want some figgy pudding,
We all want some figgy pudding,
So bring some out here!
Good tidings we bring . . .

3
We won't go until we get some,
We won't go until we get some,
We won't go until we get some,
So bring some right here!
Good tidings we bring . . .

I *Saw* Three *Ships*

Traditional

With a lilt

G Am/G G Am/G G Em A7 D7
I saw three ships come sail - ing in, *On Christ - mas Day, on Christ - mas Day;* I
G F7 E7 Am7♭5 G/D A7 D7 G
saw three ships come sail - ing in, *On Christ - mas Day in the morn - ing.*

1 I saw three ships come sailing in,
On Christmas Day, on Christmas Day;
I saw three ships come sailing in,
On Christmas Day in the morning.

2 And what was in those ships all three?
On Christmas Day, on Christmas Day;
And what was in those ships all three?
On Christmas Day in the morning.

3 Our Saviour Christ and his lady.

4 Pray, whither sailed those ships all three?

5 O they sailed into Bethlehem.

6 And all the bells on earth shall ring.

7 And all the angels in heaven shall sing.

8 And all the souls on earth shall sing.

9 Then let us all rejoice amain.

William's *Home* Coming *At* Christmas *from* Sons & Lovers *by* D. H. Lawrence

They were very poor that autumn. William had just gone away to London, and his mother missed his money. He sent ten shillings once or twice, but he had many things to pay for at first. His letter came regularly once a week. He wrote a good deal to his mother, telling her all his life, how he made friends, and was exchanging lessons with a Frenchman, how he enjoyed London. His mother felt again he was remaining to her just as when he was at home. She wrote to him every week her direct, rather witty letters. All day long, as she cleaned the house, she thought of him. He was in London: he would do well. Almost, he was like her knight who wore *her* favour in the battle.

He was coming at Christmas for five days. There had never been such preparations. Paul and Arthur scoured the land for holly and evergreens. Annie made the pretty paper hoops in the old-fashioned way. And there was unheard-of-extravagance in the larder. Mrs Morel made a big and magnificent cake. Then, feeling queenly, she showed Paul how to blanch almonds. He skinned the long nuts reverently, counting them all, to see not one was lost. It was said that eggs whisked better in a cold place. So the boy stood in the scullery, where the temperature was nearly at freezing point, and whisked and whisked, and flew in excitement to his mother as the white of egg grew stiffer and more snowy.

'Just look, mother! Isn't it lovely?'

And he balanced a bit on his nose, then blew it in the air.

'Now, don't waste it,' said the mother.

Everybody was mad with excitement. William was coming on Christmas Eve. Mrs Morel surveyed the pantry. There was a big plum cake, and a rice cake, jam tarts, lemon tarts, and mince-pies – two enormous dishes. She was finishing cooking – Spanish tarts and cheesecakes. Everywhere was decorated. The kissing bunch of berried holly hung with bright and glittering things, spun slowly over Mrs Morel's head as she

trimmed her little tarts in the kitchen. A great fire roared. There was scent of cooked pastry. He was due at seven o'clock, but he would be late. The three children had gone to meet him. She was alone. But at a quarter to seven Morel came in again. Neither wife nor husband spoke. He sat in his armchair, quite awkward with excitement, and she quietly went on with her baking. Only by the careful way in which she did things could it be told how much moved she was. The clock ticked on.

'What time dost say he's coming?' Morel asked for the fifth time.

'The train gets in at half past six,' she replied emphatically.

'Then he'll be here at ten past seven.'

'Eh, Bless you, it'll be hours late on the Midland,' she said indifferently. But she hoped, by expecting him late, to bring him early. Morel went down the entry to look for him. The he came back.

'Goodness, man!' she said. 'You're like an ill-setting hen.'

'Hadna you better be getting' him summat t'eat ready?' asked the father.

'There's plenty of time,' she answered.

'There's not much *I* can see on,' he answered, turning crossly in his chair. She began to clear the table. The kettle was singing. They waited and waited.

Meantime the three children were on the platform at Sethley Bridge, on the Midland main line, two miles from home. They waited one hour. A train came – he was not there. Down the line the red and green lights shone. It was very dark and very cold.

'Ask him if the London train's come,' said Paul to Annie, when they saw a man in a tip cap.

'I'm not,' said Annie. 'You be quiet – he might send us off.'

But Paul was dying for the man to know they were expecting someone by the London train: it sounded so grand. Yet he was much too much scared of broaching any man, let alone one in a peaked cap, to dare to ask. The three children could scarcely go into the waiting-room for the fear of being sent away, and for fear something should happen whilst they were off the platform. Still they waited in the dark and cold.

'It's an hour an' a half late,' said Arthur pathetically.

'Well' said Annie, 'it's Christmas Eve.'

They all grew silent. He wasn't coming. They looked down the darkness of the railway. There was London! It seemed the uttermost of distance. They thought anything might happen if one came from London. They were all too troubled to talk. Cold and unhappy, and silent, they huddled together on the platform.

At last, after more than two hours, they saw the lights of an engine peering round,

away down the darkness. A porter ran out. The children drew back with beating hearts. A great train bound for Manchester drew up. Two doors opened, and from one of them, William. They flew to him. He handed parcels to them cheerily, and immediately began to explain that this great train had stopped for *his* sake at such a small station as Sethley Bridge: it was not booked to stop.

Meanwhile the parents where getting anxious. The table was set, the chop was cooked, everything was ready. Mrs Morel put her on her black apron. She was wearing her best dress. Then she sat, pretending to read. The minutes were a torture to her.

'H'm!' said Morel. 'It's an hour an' a ha'ef.'

'And those children waiting!' she said.

'Th' train canna ha' come in yet,' he said.

'I tell you, on Christmas Eve they're *hours* wrong.'

They were both a bit cross with each other, so gnawed with anxiety. The ash-tree moaned outside in a cold, raw wind. And all that space of night from London home! Mrs Morel suffered. The slight click of the works inside the clock irritated her. It was getting so late; it was getting unbearable.

At last there was a sound of voices, and a footstep in the entry.

'Ha's here!' cried Morel, jumping up.

Then he stood back The mother ran a few steps towards the door and waited. There was a rush and a patter of feet, the door burst open. William was there. He dropped his Gladstone bag and took his mother in his arms.

'Mater!' he said.

'My boy!' she cried.

And for two seconds, no longer, she clasped him and kissed him. Then she withdrew and said, trying to be quite normal:

'But how late you are!'

'Aren't I!' he cried, turning to his father. 'Well, dad!'

The two men shook hands.

'Well, my lad!'

Morel's eyes were wet.

'We thought tha'd niver be commin',' he said.

'Oh, I'd come!' exclaimed William.

Then the son turned to his mother.

'But you look well,' she said proudly, laughing.

'Well' he exclaimed. 'I should think so – coming home!'

He was a fine fellow, big, straight, and fearless-looking. He looked round at the evergreens and the kissing bunch, and the little tarts that lay in their tins on the hearth.

'By jove! mother, it's not different!' he said, as if in relief.

Everybody was still for a second. Then he suddenly sprang forward, picked a tart from the hearth, and pushed it whole into his mouth.

'Well, did iver you see such a parish oven!' the father exclaimed.

He had brought them endless presents. Every penny he had he had spent on them. There was a sense of luxury overflowing in the house. For his mother there was an umbrella with gold on the pale handle. She kept it to her dying day, and would have lost anything rather than that. Everybody had something gorgeous, and besides, there were pounds of unknown sweets: Turkish delight, crystallised pineapple, and such-like things which, the children thought, only the splendour of London could provide. And Paul boasted of these sweets among his friends.

'Real pineapple, cut off in slices, and then turned into crystal – fair grand!'

Everybody was mad with happiness in the family. Home was home, and they loved it with a passion of love, whatever the suffering had been. There were parties, there were rejoicings. People came in to see William, to see what difference London had made to him. And they all found him 'such a gentlemen, and *such* a fine fellow, my word!'

December
John Clare (1793-1864)

While snows the window–panes bedim,
The fire curls up a sunny charm,
Where, creaming o'er the pitcher's rim,
The flowering ale is set to warm;
Mirth, full of joy as summer bees,
Sits there, its pleasures to impart,
And children, 'tween their parents' knees,
Sing scraps of carols o'er by heart.

And some, to view the winter weathers,
Climb up the window-seat with glee,
Likening the snow to falling feathers,
In fancy's infant ecstasy;
Laughing, with superstitious love,
O'er visions wild that youth supplies,
Of people pulling geese above,
And keeping Christmas in the skies.

As tho' the homestead trees were drest,
In lieu of snow, with dancing leaves,
As tho' the sun-dried martin's nest,
Instead of ickles, hung the eaves,
The children hail the happy day –
As if the snow were April's grass,
And pleas'd, as 'neath the warmth of May,
Sport o'er the water froze to glass.

The *Coventry* Carol

Traditional

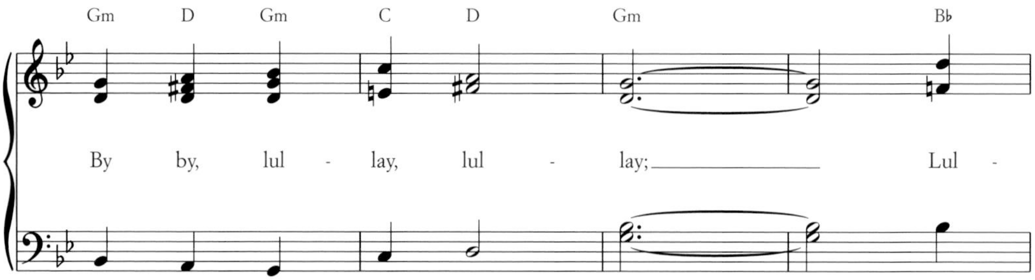

Slowly

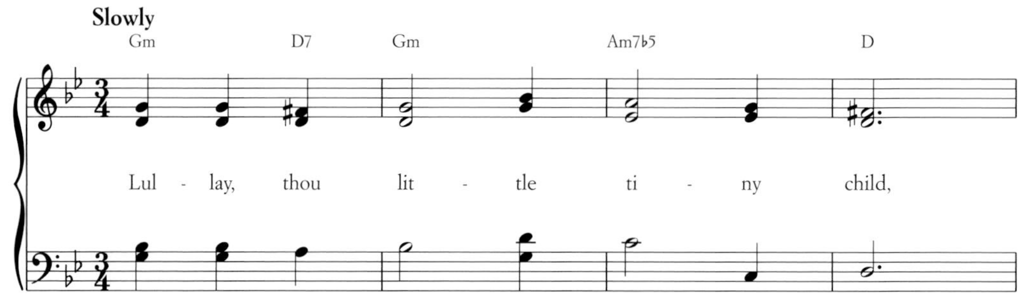

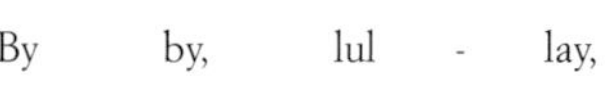

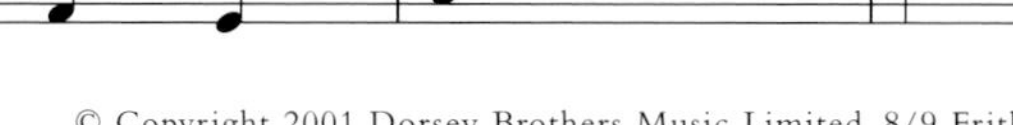

F/A
Gm
F
Gm
Am7♭5
D
- lay, thou lit - tle ti - ny child,

Gm
D
Gm
C
D
G
By by, lul - lay, lul - lay.

1 Lullay, thou little tiny child,
By by, lullay, lullay;
Lullay, thou little tiny child,
By by, lullay, lullay.

2 O sisters too, how may we do,
For to preserve this day
This poor youngling, for whom we sing
By by, lullay, lullay?

3 Herod the King in his raging,
Chargèd he hath this day
His men of might, in his own sight,
All children young to slay.

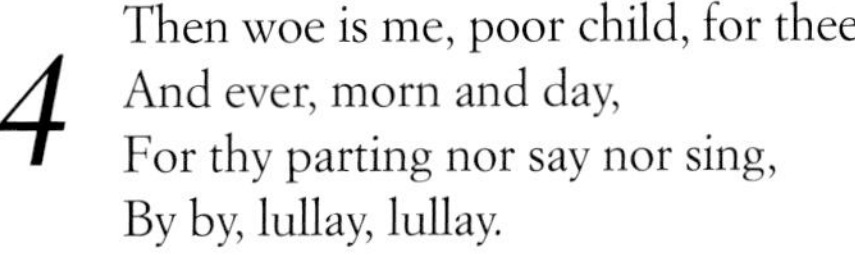

4 Then woe is me, poor child, for thee,
And ever, morn and day,
For thy parting nor say nor sing,
By by, lullay, lullay.

Unto *Us* A *Boy* Is *Born*

Traditional *English Words by* **George Woodward**

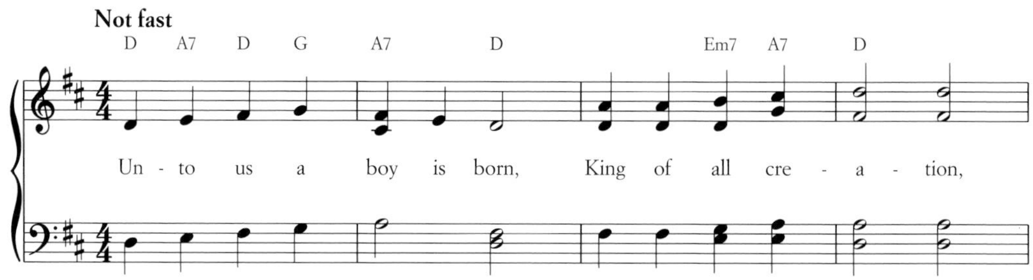

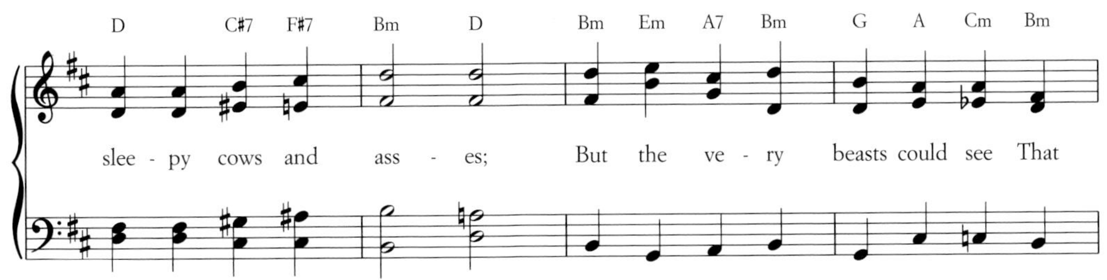

1 Unto us a boy is born,
King of all creation,
Came he to a world forlorn,
The Lord of every nation.

2 Cradled in a stall was he
With sleepy cows and asses;
But the very beasts could see
That he all men surpasses.

3 Herod then with fear was filled:
'A prince', he said 'in Jewry!'
All the little boys he killed
At Bethlem in his fury.

4 Now may Mary's Son who came
So long ago to love us,
Lead us all with hearts aflame
Unto the joys above us.

5 Omega and Alpha he!
Let the organ thunder,
While the choir with peals of glee,
Doth rend the air asunder.

The *Twelve* Days *Of* Christmas

Traditional

G C G G Am D7 G

tree. 3. On the THIRD day of Christ - mas my true love gave to me

D7 G Am G/D D7

Three French hens, two tur - tle doves, and a par - tridge in a pear

G C G G

tree. 4. On the FOURTH day of Christ - mas my

Am D7 G Am7 D7 Am7 D7

true love gave to me Four call - ing birds, three French hens,

C7 F7 D7 G Am G/D D7 G C G

two tur - tle doves, and a par - tridge in a pear tree. 5. On the

G Am D7 G Em7 A7
FIFTH day of Christ - mas my true love gave to me Five gold
D D7 G Em Am7 Em7
rings, four call - ing birds, three French hens,
A7 D G Am G/D D7 G F E♭ D7
two tur - tle doves, and a par - tridge in a pear tree. 6. On the
G Am D7 G
SIXTH
SEVENTH
EIGHTH
NINTH
TENTH
ELEVENTH
TWELFTH
day of Christ - mas my true love gave to me

Repeat this bar in reverse order as necessary

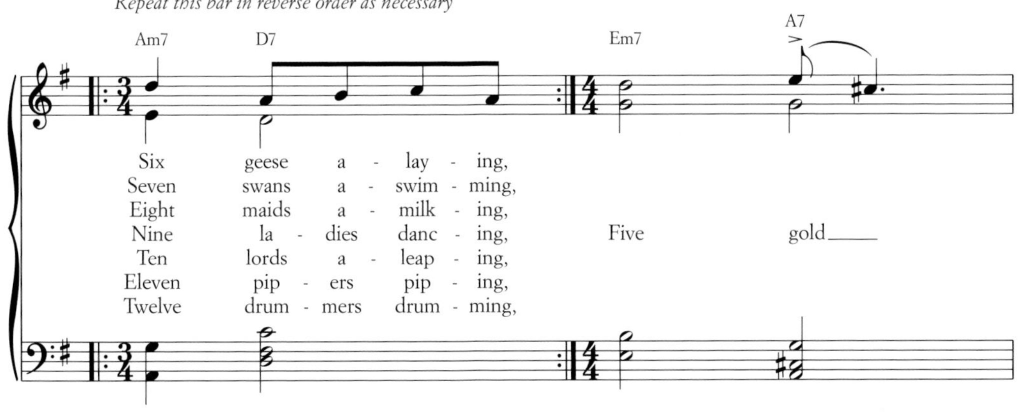
Am7 D7 Em7 A7
Six geese a - lay - ing,
Seven swans a - swim - ming,
Eight maids a - milk - ing,
Nine la - dies danc - ing,
Ten lords a - leap - ing,
Eleven pip - ers pip - ing,
Twelve drum - mers drum - ming,
Five gold

Dsus D G7 C Am7 D7 Em
rings, four call - ing birds, three French hens,

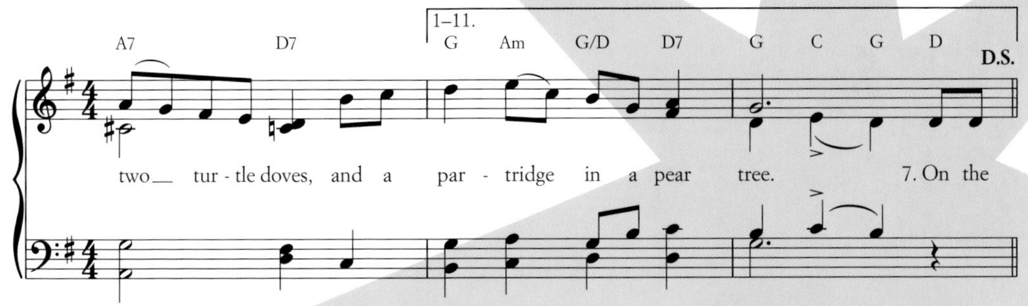
A7 D7
1–11.
G Am G/D D7 G C G D
D.S.
two tur - tle doves, and a par - tridge in a pear tree. 7. On the

12.
G C G/D D7sus D7 G
par - tridge in a pear tree.

On the FIRST day of Christmas my true love gave to me
A partridge in a pear tree.

On the SECOND day of Christmas my true love gave to me
Two turtle doves, and a partridge in a pear tree.

On the THIRD day of Christmas my true love gave to me
Three French hens, two turtle doves,
and a partridge in a pear tree.

On the FOURTH day of Christmas my true love gave to me
Four calling birds, . . .

On the FIFTH day of Christmas my true love gave to me
Five gold rings, . . .

On the SIXTH day of Christmas my true love gave to me
Six geese a-laying, . . .

On the SEVENTH day of Christmas my true love gave to me
Seven swans a-swimming, . . .

On the EIGHTH day of Christmas my true love gave to me
Eight maids a-milking, . . .

On the NINTH day of Christmas my true love gave to me
Nine ladies dancing, . . .

On the TENTH day of Christmas my true love gave to me
Ten lords a-leaping, . . .

On the ELEVENTH day of Christmas my true love gave to me
Eleven pipers piping, . . .

On the TWELFTH day of Christmas my true love gave to me
Twelve drummers drumming, eleven pipers piping,
ten lords a-leaping, nine ladies dancing,
eight maids a-milking, seven swans a-swimming,
six geese a-laying, five gold rings, four calling birds,
three French hens, two turtle doves,
and a partridge in a pear tree.

Christmas *Weather* from *Emma* by *Jane* Austen

'Christmas weather,' observed Mr Elton. 'Quite seasonable; and extremely fortunate we may think ourselves that it did not begin yesterday, and prevent this day's party, which it might very possibly have done, for Mr Woodhouse would hardly have ventured had there been much snow on the ground; but now it is of no consequence. This is quite the season indeed for friendly meetings. At Christmas everybody invites their friends about them, and people think little of even the worst weather. I was snowed up at a friend's house once for a week. Nothing could be pleasanter. I went for only one night, and could not get away till that very day's se'ennight.'

Mr John Knightley looked as if he did not comprehend the pleasure, but said only, coolly,

'I cannot wish to be snowed up a week at Randalls.'

At another time Emma might have been amused, but she was too much astonished now at Mr Elton's spirits for other feelings. Harriet seemed quite forgotten in the expectation of a pleasant party.

'We are sure of excellent fires,' continued he, 'and every thing in the greatest comfort. Charming people, Mr and Mrs Weston; – Mrs Weston indeed is much beyond praise, and he is exactly what one values, so hospitable, and so fond of society; – it will be a small party, but where small parties are select, they are perhaps the most agreeable of any. Mr Weston's dining-room does not accommodate more than ten comfortably; and for my part, I would rather under such circumstances, fall short by two than exceed by two. I think you will agree with me, (turning with a soft air to Emma,) I think I shall certainly have your approbation, though Mr Knightley perhaps, from being used to the large parties of London, may not quite enter into our feelings.'

'I know nothing of the large parties of London, sir – I never dine with anybody.'

'Indeed!' (in a tone of wonder and pity,) 'I had no idea that the law had been so great a slavery. Well, sir, the time must come when you will be paid for all of this, when you will have little labour and great enjoyment.'

'My first enjoyment,' replied John Knightley, as they passed through the sweep-gate, 'will be to find myself safe at Hartfield again.'

Angels *From* The *Realms* Of *Glory*

Music: **Traditional** *Words by* **James Montgomery**

Lively

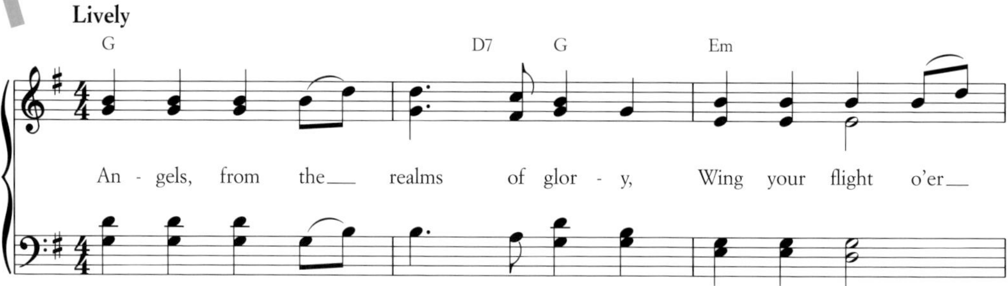
G
D7
G
Em
An - gels, from the realms of glor - y, Wing your flight o'er

Am7
D7
G
D7
G
Em
G7
all the earth; Ye, who sang cre - a - tion's sto - ry, Now pro - claim Mes -

C
D7
G
Bm7
E7
Am7
D7
- si - ah's birth: *Come*

Gmaj7 C Am7 D7sus D7 Em D/F♯ G Am7 G/D D

_____ and_ wor - ship, Christ, the new - born King;___

Bm7 E7 Am7 D7 Gmaj7 C

Come_____ and_

A7 D7sus D7 Em D/F♯ G Am G/D D7 G

wor - ship, Wor - ship Christ the new - born King.

1 Angels, from the realms of glory,
Wing your flight o'er all the earth;
Ye, who sang creation's story,
Now proclaim Messiah's birth:

Come and worship,
Christ, the newborn King;
Come and worship,
Worship Christ the newborn King.

2 Shepherds in the field abiding,
Watching o'er your flocks by night,
God with man is now residing;
Yonder shines the infant light:
Come and worship . . .

3 Sages, leave your contemplations;
Brighter visions beam afar;
Seek the great Desire of Nations;
Ye have seen his natal star:
Come and worship . . .

4 Saints before the altar bending,
Watching long in hope and fear;
Suddenly the Lord, descending,
In his temple shall appear:
Come and worship . . .

5 Though an infant now we view him,
He shall fill his Father's throne,
Gather all the nations round him,
Every knee shall then bow down:
Come and worship . . .

Good *King* Wenceslas

Music: **Traditional** *Words by* ***John Neale***

Lively
G Am7 G/B Am/C G/B Am7 G C G C D7
Good King Wen - ces - las looked out On the Feast of
Gsus G Em C G Am G/B A7 D7sus D7 C G C D7
Ste - phen, When the snow lay round a - bout, Deep and crisp and

C/G G G/B C Baug B7 Em B7 Em
e - ven: Bright - ly shone the moon that night,

C G C D7 Gsus G C7 G/D A7 D7
Though the frost was cru - el, When a poor man

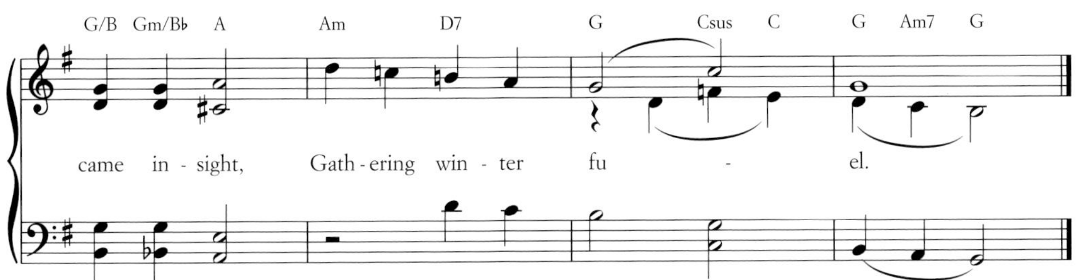
G/B Gm/B♭ A Am D7 G Csus C G Am7 G
came in - sight, Gath - ering win - ter fu - el.

Good King Wenceslas looked out
On the Feast of Stephen,
When the snow lay round about,
1 Deep and crisp and even:
Brightly shone the moon that night,
Though the frost was cruel,
When a poor man came in sight,
Gathering winter fuel.

'Hither page, and stand by me,
If though knowst it, telling,
Yonder peasant, who is he?
2 Where and what his dwelling?'
'Sire, he lives a good league hence,
Underneath the mountain,
Right against the forest fence,
By Saint Agnes' fountain.'

'Bring me flesh and bring me wine,
Bring me pine-logs hither:
Thou and I will see him dine
3 When we bear them thither.'
Page and monarch, forth they went,
Forth they went together;
Through the rude wind's wild lament
And the bitter weather.

'Sire, the night is darker now,
And the wind grows stronger;
Fails my heart, I know not how;
4 I can go no longer.'
'Mark my footsteps, good my page;
Tread thou in them boldly:
Thou shalt find the winter's rage
Freeze thy blood less coldly.'

In his master's steps he trod,
Where the snow lay dinted;
Heat was in the very sod
5 Which the Saint had printed.
Therefore, Christian men, be sure,
Wealth or rank possessing,
Ye who now will bless the poor,
Shall yourselves find blessing.

Mulled *Wine*

Ingredients...

5 bottles red wine

6oz (170g) sugar

15 cloves

3 handfuls sultanas

$\frac{1}{2}$ tumbler of brandy or more!

Simmer gently, adding sugar gradually, to taste. Serve hot.

Truffles

Ingredients...

$1\frac{1}{2}$oz (40g) shelled walnuts

4oz (110g) plain chocolate

$1\frac{1}{2}$oz (40g) finely chopped cherries

2oz (60g) margarine

1 egg yolk

1-2 teaspoons of rum, brandy or liqueur

desiccated coconut

Melt chocolate and margarine in a bowl and beat till smooth.
Add other ingredients & mix. Leave in fridge to set.
Make into little balls and toss in coconut. Put into sweet cases.

Victorian *Christmas* Pudding

Ingredients...

6oz (170g) fresh white breadcrumbs

2oz (60g) plain flour

8oz (220g) suet *(preferably vegetarian suet)*

8oz (220g) plump Californian raisins

8oz (220g) currants

8oz (220g) soft brown sugar

2oz (60g) candied peel *(optional)*

2oz (60g) chopped flake almonds

1 grated nutmeg

grated rind and juice of one orange and one lemon

1 level teaspoon of salt

4 free range eggs, lightly beaten

1 wine glass *each* of sherry and brandy *(size of wine glass depends on how 'boozy' you like your puddings)*

Put all ingredients in large mixing bowl and mix together. Gradually stir in the juice, beaten eggs, wine and brandy. Cut a small circle of greaseproof paper to fit the bottom of the pudding basin (stops puddings sticking when turned out onto serving plate). Fill to within 1 inch (3 cm) of the top of basin. Place another large circle of greaseproof paper on top of the pudding, cover with large piece of foil or muslin.

Steam puddings for at least 5 hours (they will need at least another 1-2 hours steaming on Christmas day). On the big day, turn out onto serving dish, pour warmed brandy over the pudding and light – once flames have disappeared serve with double cream, brandy sauce (or brandy butter) and enjoy!

Christmas *Cake*

Ingredients...

12oz (340g) plain flour

10oz (280g) butter

10oz (280g) sugar

½ teaspoon each of mixed spice, mace, cinnamon

1 tablespoon black treacle

5 eggs

1½ lbs (680g) currants

12oz (340g) raisins

12oz (340g) sultanas

4oz (110g) chopped blanched almonds

4oz (110g) chopped cherries

finely grated rind of a lemon and a orange

6oz (170g) mixed crystalline peel

a pinch of salt

Cream together butter, sugar and treacle until soft and light in texture.
Sieve all dry ingredients.
Mix all fruit together.
Beat eggs and stir them and the flour mixture alternately into butter mix.
Add fruit and mix well.
Bake for about 4½ hours at gas mark 3 in a 9 inch (20 cm) tin.
Spike when cool and add brandy.

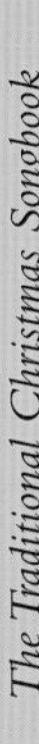

Scotch *Black* Bun

A traditional Scottish Christmas cake

Ingredients...

1lb (450g) blue raisins

1lb (450g) sultanas

2lbs (900g) currants

4oz (110g) peel

8oz (220g) almonds

1/2 oz (15g) ground ginger

1/2 oz (15g) ground cinnamon

1/2 oz (15g) Jamaica pepper

1/2 teaspoon black pepper

1 teaspoon baking soda

1 teaspoon cream of tartar

8oz (220g) sugar

Mix all ingredients with a large egg.

For the bun crust...

1 1/2 cups of flour (190g)

4 oz butter (110g)

1/2 teaspoon baking powder

Rub butter into flour and mix to a firm paste with water. Roll out into a thin sheet and line a tin, fill with fruit mixture and put on a crust lid. Bake in a hot oven for 30-40 minutes until golden. Store in a cool dry place for Christmas.

Ding *Dong* Merrily *On* High

Music: **Traditional** *Words by* **George Woodward**

Brightly

G Am/G D7 G C D7sus D7 G
Ding dong! mer - ri - ly on high, in heaven the bells are ring - ing,

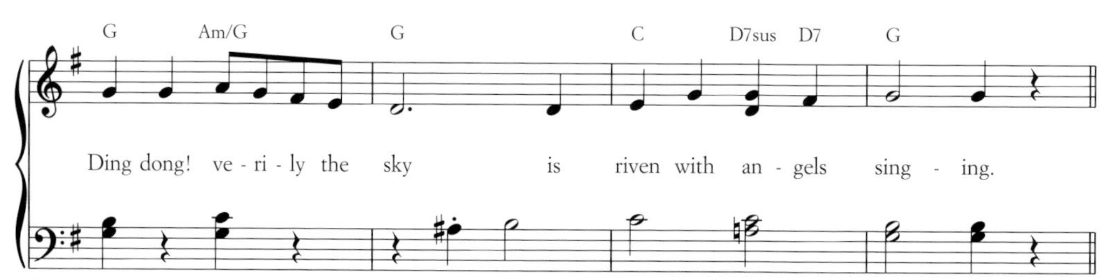
G Am/G G C D7sus D7 G
Ding dong! ve - ri - ly the sky is riven with an - gels sing - ing.

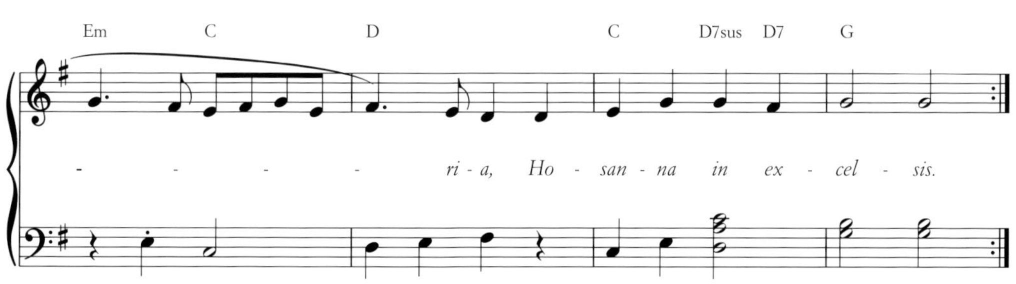

1 Ding dong! merrily on high, in heaven the bells are ringing,
Ding dong! verily the sky is riven with angels singing.

Gloria, Hosanna in excelsis.

2 E'en so here below, below, let steeple bells be swungen,
And io, io, io, by priest and people sungen.
Gloria . . .

3 Pray you, dutifully prime your matin chime, you ringers;
May you beautifully rhyme your eve-time song, you singers.
Gloria . . .

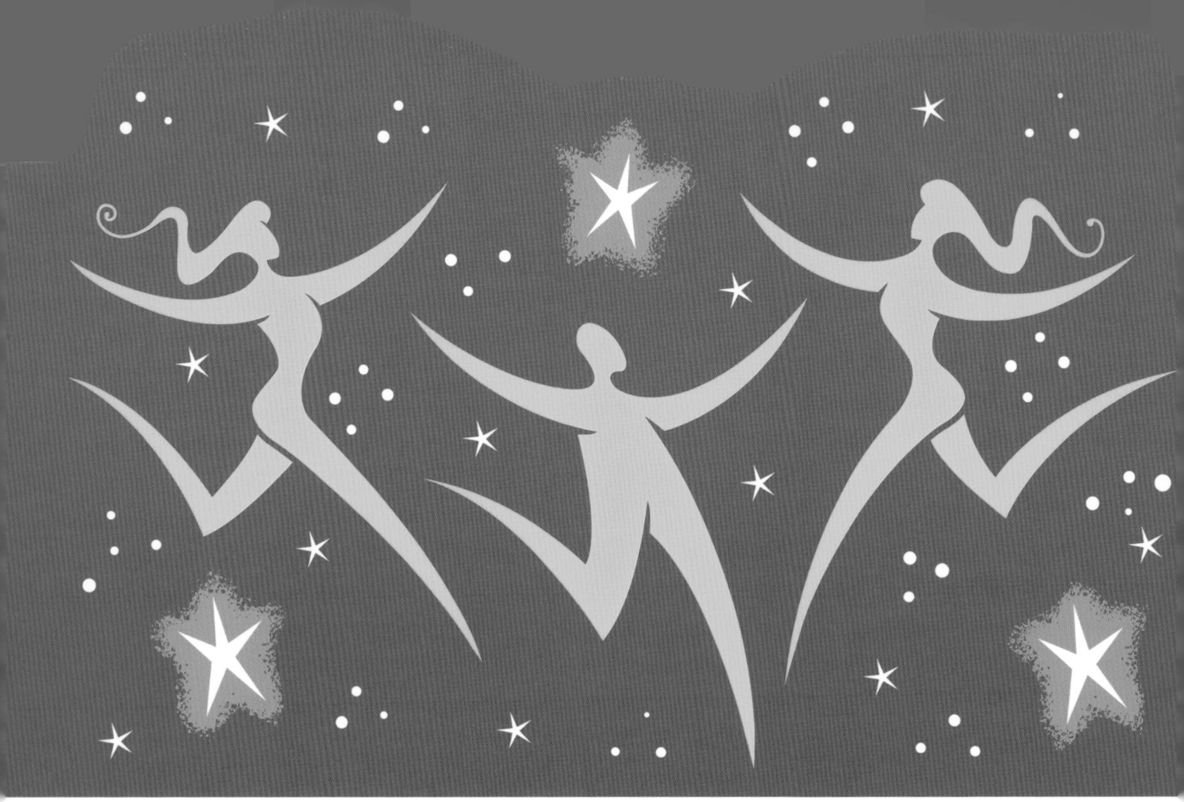

Tomorrow *Shall* Be *My* Dancing *Day*

Traditional

Lively dance tempo

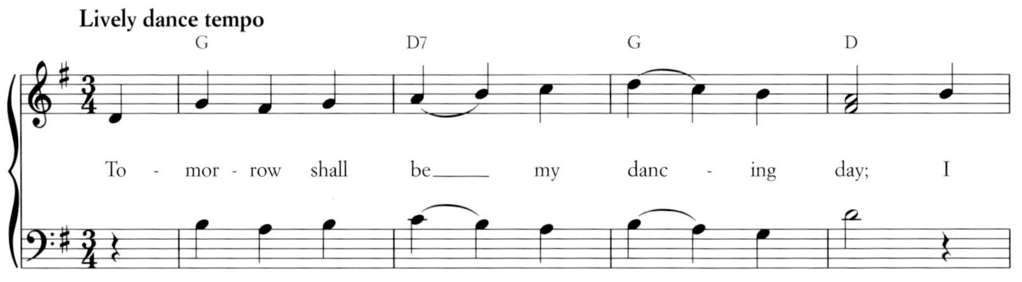

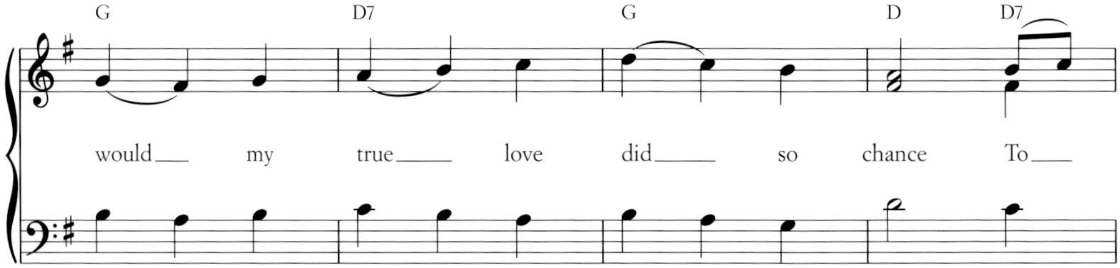

G D7 G D D7

would___ my true___ love did___ so chance To___

1 Tomorrow shall be my dancing day;
I would my true love did so chance
To see the legend of my play,
To call my true love to the dance.

Sing O my love, O my love, my love, my love;
This have I done for my true love.

2 Then was I born of a Virgin pure,
Of her I took my fleshly substance,
Thus was I knit to man's nature,
To call my true love to the dance.
Sing O my love . . .

3 In a manger laid and wrapped I was,
So very poor, this was my chance,
Betwixt an ox and a silly poor ass,
To call my true love to my dance.
Sing O my love . . .

Christians *Awake*

Words by **John Byrom** *Music by* ***John Wainwright***

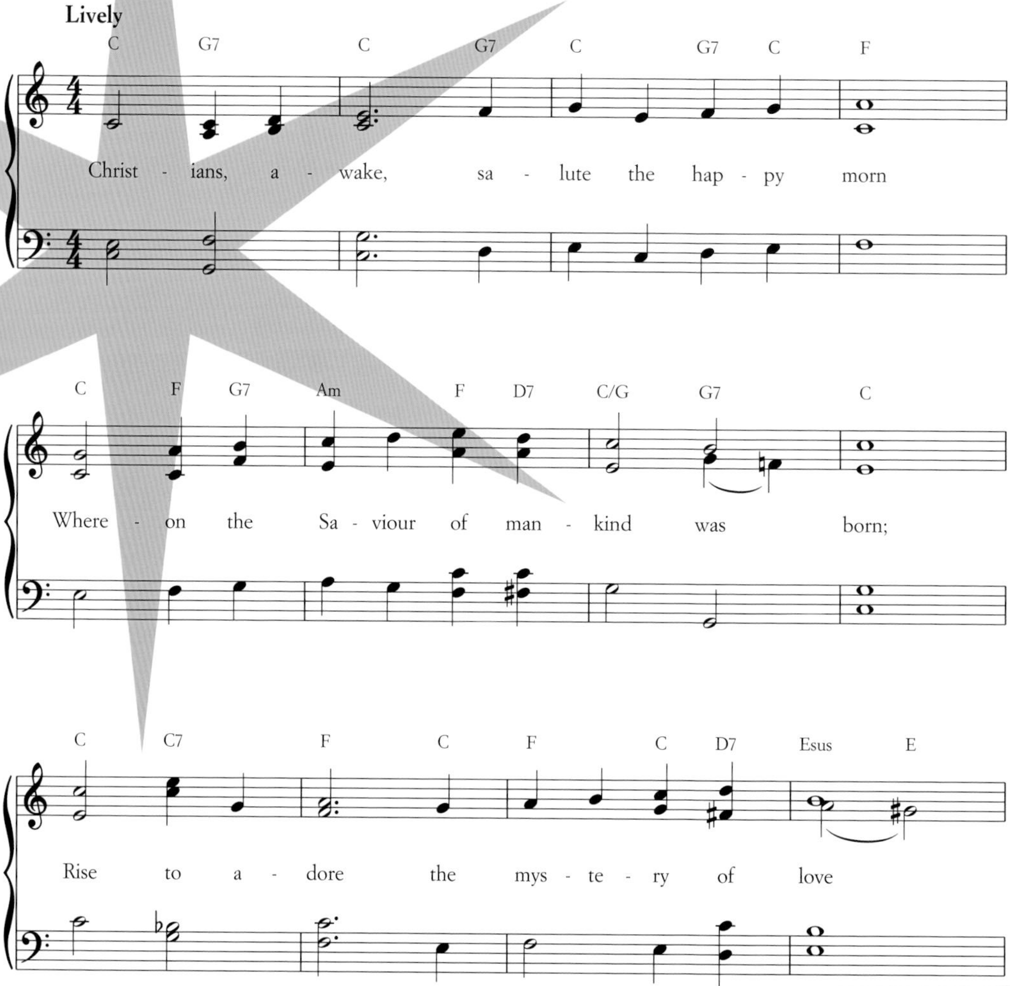

Lively
C G7 C G7 C G7 C F
Christ - ians, a - wake, sa - lute the hap - py morn
C F G7 Am F D7 C/G G7 C
Where - on the Sa - viour of man - kind was born;
C C7 F C F C D7 Esus E
Rise to a - dore the mys - te - ry of love

E Am E F Bm♭5 Am/E E7 Am
Which hosts of an - gels chan - ted from a - bove;

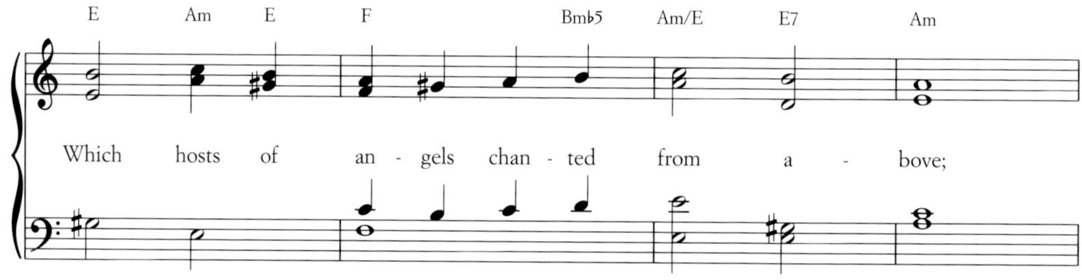

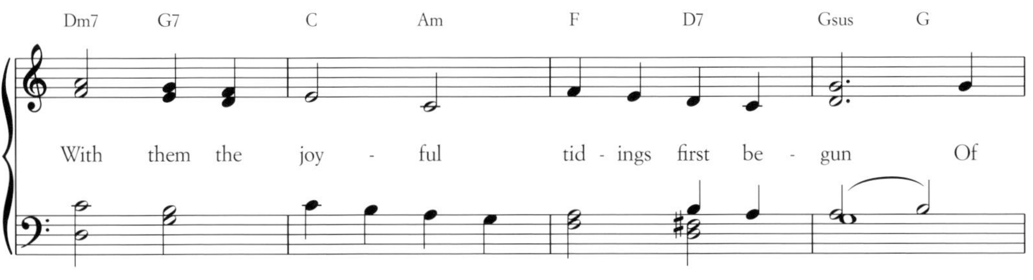

1 Christians awake, salute the happy morn
Whereon the Saviour of mankind was born;
Rise to adore the mystery of love
Which hosts of angels chanted from above;
With them the joyful tidings first begun
Of God incarnate and the Virgin's Son.

2 Then to the watchful shepherds it was told,
Who heard the angelic herald's voice:
'Behold, I bring good tidings of a Saviour's birth
To you and all the nations upon earth;
This day hath God fulfilled his promised word,
This day is born a Saviour, Christ the Lord.'

3 He spake; and straightway the celestial choir
In hymns of joy, unknown before, conspire.
The praises of redeeming love they sang,
And heaven's whole orb with Alleluias rang;
God's highest glory was their anthem still,
Peace upon earth, and mutual goodwill.

4 O may we keep and ponder in our mind
God's wondrous love in saving lost mankind;
Trace we the Babe, who hath retrieved our loss,
From the poor manger to the bitter cross;
Tread in his steps, assisted by his grace,
Till man's first heavenly state again takes place.

5 Then may we hope, the angelic hosts among,
To sing, redeemed, a glad triumphal song;
He that was born upon this joyful day
Around us all his glory shall display;
Saved by his love, incessant we shall sing
Eternal praise to heaven's almighty King.

Past *Three* O'Clock

Words: **Traditional** *Music by* **George Woodward**

Moderately
G C G D7 G Em D7 D♯dim
Past three a clock, And a cold__ fros - ty morn - ing,

Em C G Gm A7 D7 G
Past three a clock; Good mor - row, mas - ters all!

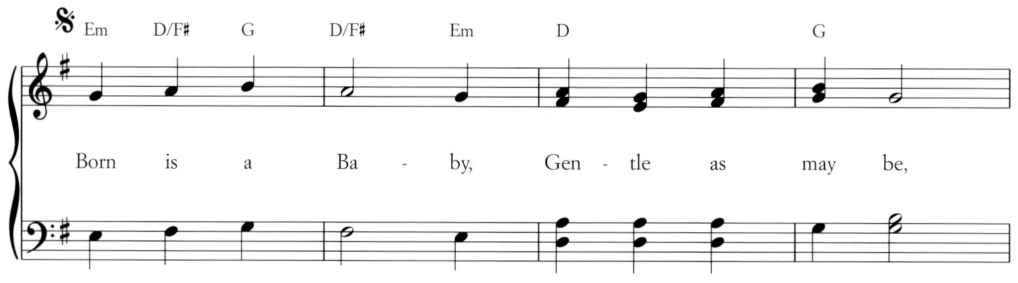
Em D/F♯ G D/F♯ Em D G
Born is a Ba - by, Gen - tle as may be,

Past three a clock
And a cold frosty morning,
Past three a clock;
Good morrow masters all!

1
Born is a Baby,
Gentle as may be,
Son of the eternal
Father supernal.
Past three a clock . . .

2
Seraph quire singeth,
Angel bell ringeth;
Hark how they rime it,
Time it and chime it.
Past three a clock . . .

3
Mid earth rejoices
Hearing such voices
Ne'ertofore so well
Carolling *Nowell.*
Past three a clock . . .

4
Light out of star-land
Leadeth from far land
Princes, to meet him,
Worship and greet him.
Past three a clock . . .

5
Myrrh from full coffer,
Incense they offer;
Nor is the golden
Nugget witholden.
Past three a clock . . .

6
Thus they: I pray you,
Up, sirs, nor stay you
Till ye confess him
Likewise, and bless him.
Past three a clock . . .

Patapan

Traditional

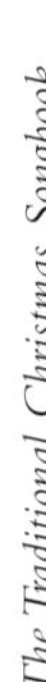

Light and rhythmic

1 Take thy tabor and thy flute,
None today must e'er be mute:
With such jolly shepherd toys,
Tu-re-lu-re-lu, pa-ta-pa-ta-pan;
To the sound of this shrill noise,
Let us raise a Nowell, boys!

2 Long ago our fathers sang
Such a song on this same day:
'Twas of Bethlehem, their lay,
Tu-re-lu-re-lu, pa-ta-pa-ta-pan;
Where wise kings and shepherds stray
To the stars their music rang.

3 As we join our choicest airs,
In a hymn that upward fares:
Earth and heaven seem near our prayers:
Tu-re-lu-re-lu, pa-ta-pa-ta-pan;
Vanish all our daily cares
While we dance and sing Nowell.

The *Thieves* Who *Couldn't* Help *Sneezing* *by* Thomas *Hardy*

Many years ago, when oak trees now past their prime were about as large as elderly gentlemen's walking-sticks, there lived in Wessex a yeoman's son, whose name was Hubert. He was about fourteen years of age, and was as remarkable for his candour and lightness of heart as for his physical courage, of which, indeed, he was a little vain. One cold Christmas Eve his father, having no other help at hand, sent him on an important errand to a small town several miles from home. He travelled on horseback, and was detained by the business till a late hour of the evening. At last, however, it was completed; he returned to the inn, the horse was saddled, and he started on his way. His journey homeward lay through the Vale of Blackmore a fertile but somewhat lonely district, with heavy clay roads and crooked lanes. In those days, too, a great part of it was thickly wooded.

It must have been about nine o'clock when, riding among the amid the overhanging trees upon his stout legged cob, Jerry, and singing a Christmas carol, to be in harmony with the seasons, Hubert fancied that he heard a noise among the boughs. This recalled to his mind that the spot he was traversing bore an evil name. Men had been waylaid there. He looked at Jerry, and wished he had been of any other colour apart from light grey; for on his account the docile animal's form was visible even there in the dense shade.

'What do I care?' he said aloud, after a few minutes of reflection.

'Jerry's legs are too nimble to any allow any highwaymen to come near me.'

'Ha! Ha! indeed,' was said in a deep voice; and the next moment a man darted from the thicket on his left hand, and another from a tree-trunk a few yards ahead. Hubert's bridle was seized, he was pulled from his horse, and although he struck out with all his might, as a brave boy would naturally do, he was overpowered. His arms were tied behind him, his legs bound tightly together, and he was thrown in a ditch. The robbers, whose faces he could now dimly perceive to be artificially blackened, at once departed, leading off the horse.

As soon as Hubert had a little recovered himself, he found that by great exertion he was to extricate his legs from the cord; but, in spite of every endeavour, his arms remained bound as fast as before. All, therefore, that he could do was to rise to his feet and proceed on his way with his arms behind him, and trust to chance for getting them unfastened. He knew that it would be impossible to reach home on foot that night, and in such a condition; but he walked on. Owing to the confusion which this attack caused in his brain, he lost his way, and would have been inclined to lie down and rest till morning among the dead leaves had he not known the danger of sleeping without wrappers in a frost so severe. So he wandered farther onwards, his arms wrung and numbed by the cord which pinioned him, and his heart aching for the loss of poor Jerry, who never had been known to kick, or bite, or show a single vicious habit. He was not a little glad when he discerned through the trees a distant light. Towards this he made his way, and presently found himself in front of a large mansion with flanking wings, gables, and towers, the battlements and chimneys showing their shapes against the stars.

All was silent; but the door stood wide open, it being from this door that the light shone which had attracted him. On entering he found himself in a vast apartment arranged as a dining-hall, and brilliantly illuminated. The walls were covered with a great deal of dark wainscoting, formed into moulded panels, carvings, closet-doors, and the usual fittings of a house of that kind. But what drew his attention most was the large table in the midst of the hall, upon which was spread a sumptuous supper, as yet untouched. Chairs were placed around, and it appeared as if something had occurred to interrupt the meal just at the time when all were ready to begin.

Even had Hubert been so inclined, he could not have eaten in his helpless state, unless by dipping his mouth into the dishes, like a pig or cow. He wished first to obtain assistance; and was about to penetrate farther into the house for that purpose when he heard hasty footsteps in the porch and the words, 'Be quick!' uttered in the deep voice which had reached him when he was dragged from the horse. There was only just time for him to dart under the table before three men entered the dining-hall. Peeping from beneath the hanging edges of the tablecloth, he perceived that their faces, too, were blackened, which at once removed any doubts he may have felt that these were the same thieves.

'Now, then,' said the first – the man with the deep voice – 'let us hide ourselves. They will all be back again in a minute. That was a good trick to get them out of the house – eh?'

'Yes. You well imitated the cries of a man in distress,' said the second.

'Excellently,' said the third.

'But they will soon find out that it was a false alarm. Come, where shall we hide? It must be some place we can stay in for two or three hours, till all are in bed and asleep. Ah! I have it. Come this way! I have learnt that the farther cupboard is not opened once in a twelve-month; it will serve our purpose exactly.'

The speaker advanced into a corridor which led from the hall. Creeping a little farther forward, Hubert could discern that the cupboard stood at the end, facing the dining-hall. The thieves entered it, and closed the door. Hardly breathing, Hubert glided forward, to learn a little more of their intention, if possible; and, coming close, he could hear the robbers whispering about the different rooms where the jewels, plate, and other valuables of the house were kept, which they plainly meant to steal.

They had not been long in hiding when a gay chattering of ladies and gentlemen was audible on the terrace without. Hubert felt that it would not do to be caught prowling about the house, unless he wished to be taken for a robber himself, and stood in a dark corner of the porch where he could see everything without being himself seen. In a moment or two a whole troop of personages came gliding past him into the house. There were an elderly gentlemen and lady, eight or nine young ladies, as many men, besides half a dozen menservants and maids. The mansion had apparently been quite emptied of its occupants.

'Now, children and young people, we will resume our meal,' said the old gentlemen. 'What the noise could have been I cannot understand. I never felt so certain in my life that there was a person being murdered outside my door.'

Then the ladies began saying how frightened they had been, and how they had expected an adventure, and how it had ended in nothing after all.

'Wait a while,' said Hubert to himself. 'You'll have adventure enough by-and-by, ladies.'

It appeared that the young men and women were married sons and daughters of the old couple, who had come that day to spend Christmas with their parents.

The door was then closed, Hubert being left outside in the porch. He thought this a proper moment for asking their assistance; and, since he was unable to knock with his hands, began boldly to kick the door.

'Hullo! What disturbance are you making here?' said a footman who opened it; and, seizing Hubert by the shoulder, he pulled him into the dining-hall. 'Here's a strange boy I have found making a noise in the porch, Sir Simon.' Everybody turned.

'Bring him forward,' said Sir Simon, the old gentleman before mentioned. 'What were you doing there, my boy?'

'Why, his arms are tied!' said one of the ladies.

'Poor fellow!' said another.

Hubert at once began to explain that he had been waylaid on his journey home, robbed of his horse, and mercilessly left in this condition by the thieves.

'Only to think of it!' exclaimed Sir Simon.

'That's a likely story,' said one of the gentlemen-guests, incredulously.

'Doubtful, hey?' asked Sir Simon.

'Perhaps he's a robber himself,' suggested a lady.

'There is a curiously wild wicked look about him, certainly, now that I examine him closely,' said the old mother.

Hubert blushed with shame; and, instead of continuing his story, and relating that robbers were concealed in the house, he doggedly held his tongue, and half resolved to let them find out their danger for themselves.

'Well, untie him,' said Sir Simon. 'Come, since it is Christmas Eve, we'll treat him well. Here, my lad; sit down in that empty at the bottom of the table, and make as good a meal as you can. When you have had your fill we will listen to more particulars of your story.'

Then feast then proceeded; and Hubert, now at liberty, was not at all sorry to join in. The more they ate and drank the merrier did the company become; the wine flowed freely, the logs flared up the chimney, the ladies laughed at the gentlemen's stories; in short, all went as noisily and as happily as a Christmas gathering in old times possibly could do.

Hubert, in spite of his hurt feelings at their doubts of his honesty, could not help being warmed both in mind and in body by the good cheer, the scene, and the example of hilarity set by his neighbours. At last he laughed as heartily at their stories and repartees as the old Baronet, Sir Simon, himself.

When the meal was almost over one of the sons, who had drunk a little too much wine, after the manner of men in that century, said to Hubert, 'Well, my boy, how are you? Can you take a pinch of snuff?' He held out one of the snuff-boxes which were then becoming common among young and old throughout the country.

'Thank you,' said Hubert, accepting a pinch.

'Tell the ladies who you are, what you are made of, and what you can do,' the young man continued, slapping Hubert upon the shoulder.

'Certainly,' said our hero, drawing himself up, and thinking it best to put a bold face on the matter. 'I am a travelling magician.'

'Indeed!'

'What shall we hear next?'

'Can you call up spirits from the vastly deep, young wizard?'

'I can conjure up a tempest in a cupboard,' Hubert replied.

'Ha-ha!' said the old Baronet, pleasantly rubbing his hands.

'We must see this performance. Girls, don't go away: here's something to be seen.'

'Not dangerous, I hope?' said the old lady.

Hubert rose from the table. 'Hand me your snuff-box, please,' he said to the young man who had made free with him. 'And now,' he continued, 'without the least noise, follow me. If any of you speak it will break the spell.'

They promised obedience. He entered the corridor, and, taking off his shoes, went on tiptoe to the cupboard door, the guests advancing in a silent group at a little distance behind him. Hubert next placed a stool in front of the door, and, by standing upon it, was tall enough to reach the top. He then, just as noiselessly, poured all the snuff from the box along the upper edge of the door, and with a few short puffs of breath, blew the snuff through the chink into the interior of the cupboard. He held up his finger to the assembly, that they might be silent.

'Dear me, what's that? said the old lady, after a minute or two had elapsed.

A suppressed sneeze had come from inside the cupboard. Hubert held up his finger again.

'How very singular,' whispered Sir Simon. 'This is most interesting.'

Hubert took advantage of the moment to gently slide the bolt of the cupboard door into its place. 'More snuff,' he said, calmly.

'More snuff,' said Sir Simon. Two or three gentlemen passed their boxes, and the contents were blown in at the top of the cupboard. Another sneeze, not quite so well suppressed as the first, was heard: then another, which seemed to say that it would not be suppressed under any circumstances whatever. At length there arose a perfect storm of sneezes.

'Excellent, excellent for one so young!' said Sir Simon. 'I am much interested in this trick of throwing the voice – called, I believe, ventriloquism.'

'More snuff', said Hubert

'More snuff', said Sir Simon. Sir Simon's man brought a large jar of the best scented Scotch.

Hubert once more charged the upper chink of the cupboard, and blew the snuff into the interior, as before. Again he charged, and again, emptying the whole contents of the jar. The tumult of sneezes became really extraordinary to listen to – there was no cessation. It was like wind, rain, and sea battling in a hurricane.

'I believe there are men inside, and that it is no trick at all!' exclaimed Sir Simon, the truth flashing on him.

'There are,' said Hubert. 'They are come to rob the house; and they are the same who stole my horse.'

The sneezes changed to spasmodic groans. One of the thieves, hearing Hubert's voice, cried, 'Oh! mercy! mercy! let us out of this!'

'Where's my horse?' cried Hubert.

'Tied to the tree in the hollow behind Short's Gibbet. Mercy! mercy! let us out, or we shall die of suffocation!'

All the Christmas guests now perceived that this was no longer sport, but serious earnest. Guns and cudgels were procured; all the menservants were called in, and arranged in position outside the cupboard. At a signal Hubert withdrew the bolt, and stood on the defensive. But the three robbers, far from attacking them, were found crouching in the corner, gasping for breath. They made no resistance; and, being pinioned, were placed in an outhouse till the morning.

Hubert now gave the remainder of his story to the assembled company, and was profusely thanked for the services he had rendered. Sir Simon pressed him to stay over the night, and accept the use of the best bedroom the house afforded, which had been occupied by Queen Elizabeth and King Charles successively when on their visits to this part of the country. But Hubert declined, being anxious to find his horse Jerry, and to test the truth of the robbers' statements concerning him.

Several of the guests accompanied Hubert to the spot behind the gibbet, alluded to by the thieves as where Jerry was hidden. When they reached the knoll and looked over, behold! there the horse stood, uninjured, and quite unconcerned. At sight of Hubert he neighed joyfully: and nothing could exceed Hubert's gladness at finding him. He mounted, wished his friends 'Good night!' and cantered off in the direction they pointed out, reaching home safely about four o'clock in the morning.

Silent *Night*

Words by **Joseph Mohr** *Music by* **Franz Gruber**

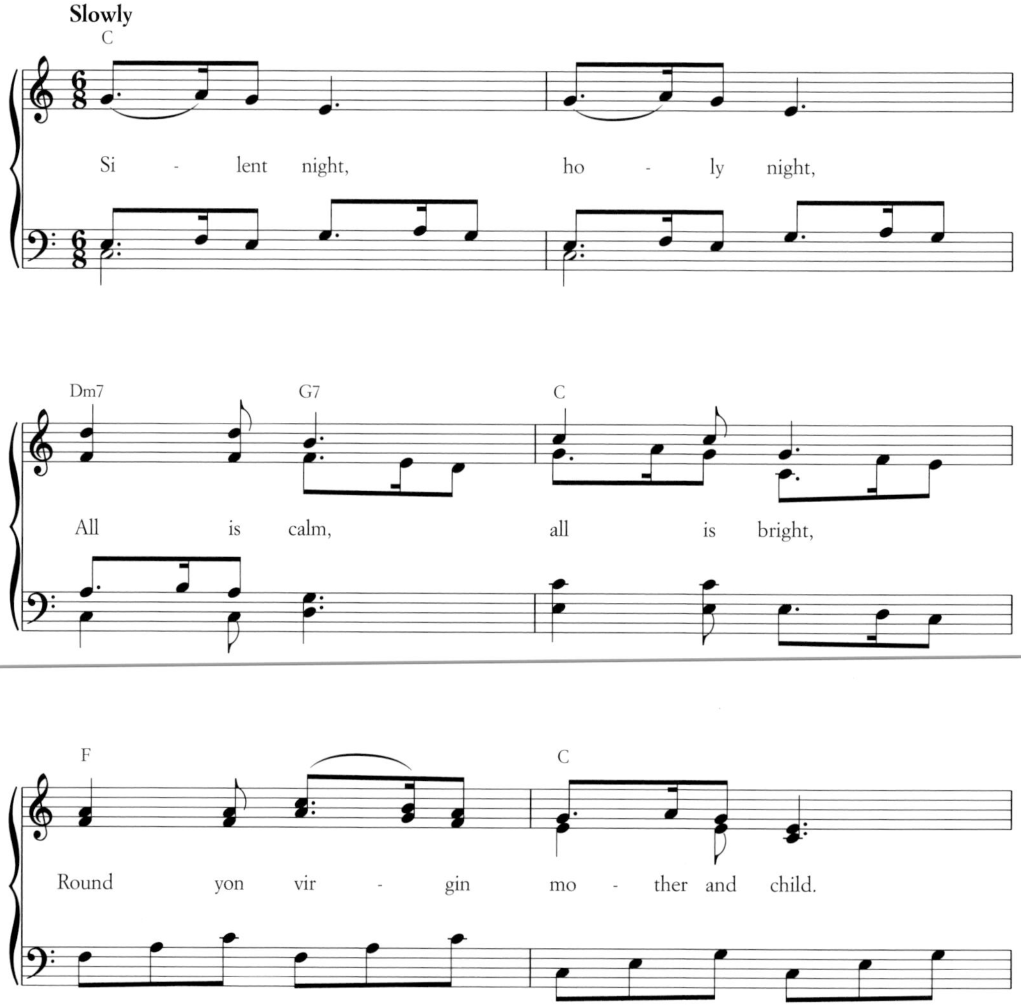

Slowly

C

Si - lent night, ho - ly night,

Dm7 G7 C

All is calm, all is bright,

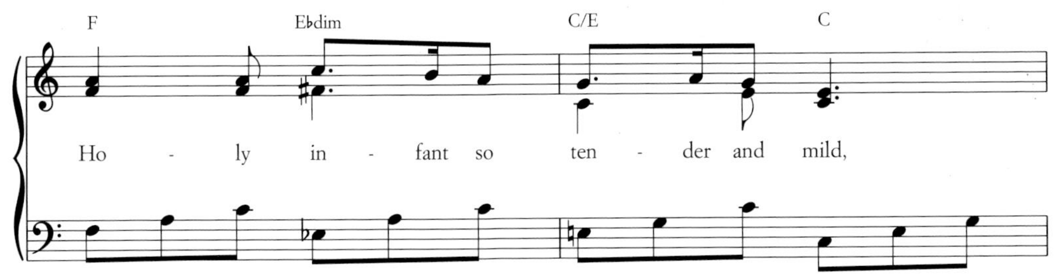

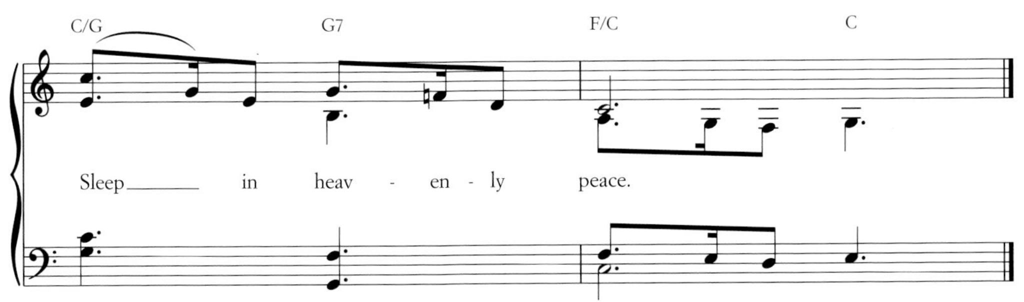

1 Silent night, holy night,
All is calm, all is bright,
Round yon virgin mother and child.
Holy infant so tender and mild,
Sleep in heavenly peace,
Sleep in heavenly peace.

2 Silent night, holy night,
Shepherds first saw the light,
Heard resounding clear and long,
Far and near, the angel song:
Christ the Saviour is here,
Christ the Saviour is here.

3 Silent night, holy night,
Son of God, oh, how bright
Love is smiling from thy face,
Peals for us the hour of grace.
Christ our Saviour is born,
Christ our Saviour is born.

Here *We* Come *A-Wassailing*

Traditional

Brightly
D
Here we come a - was - sail - ing A - mong the leaves so

D G D Bm7 Em A7
green, Here we come a - wan - d'ring So fair to be

A7 D G D G
seen. Love and joy come to you, and to you your was - sail

© Copyright 2001 Dorsey Brothers Music Limited, 8/9 Frith Street, London W1.
All Rights Reserved. International Copyright Secured.

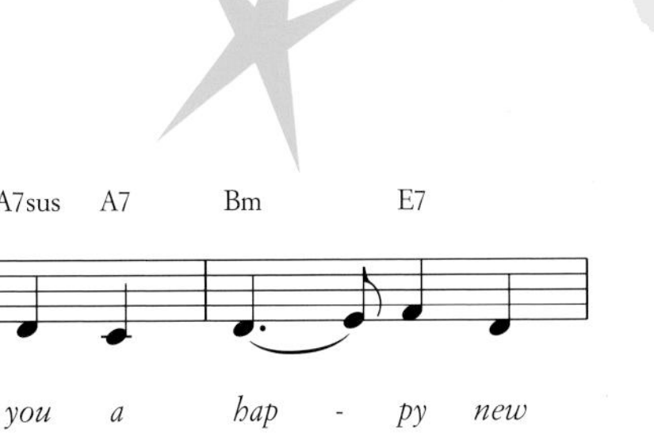

D A/G D/F# Bm Em A7sus A7 Bm E7

too And God bless you and send___ you a hap - py new

1 Here we come a-wassailing
Among the leaves so green,
Here we come a-wandering
So fair to be seen.

Love and joy come to you,
And to you your wassail too,
And God bless you and send you
a happy new year,
And God send you a happy new year.

2 Our wassail cup is made
Of the rosemary tree,
And so is your beer
Of the best barley.
Love and joy come to you . . .

3 We are not daily beggars
That beg from door to door,
But we are neighbours' children
Whom you have seen before.
Love and joy come to you . . .

4 Good master and good mistress,
As you sit by the fire,
Pray think of us poor children
Who are wandering in the mire.
Love and joy come to you . . .

5 We have a little purse
Made of ratching leather skin;
We want some of your small change
To line it well within.
Love and joy come to you . . .

In *Dulci* Jubilo

Traditional *English Words by* **R.L. Pearsall**

Moderately

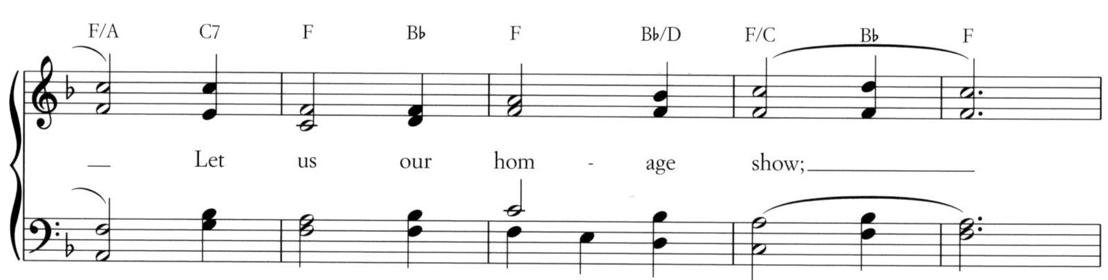

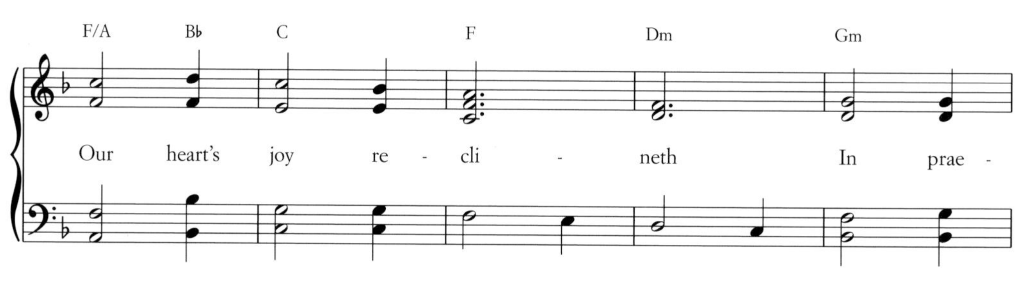

1 In dulci jubilo
Let us our homage show;
Our heart's joy reclineth
In praesepio,
And like a bright star shineth
Matris in gremio;
Alpha es et O,
Alpha es et O!

2 O Jesu parvule!
My heart is sore for thee!
Hear me, I beseech thee,
O puer optime!
My prayer let it reach thee
O Princeps gloriae!
Trahe me post te!
Trahe me post te!

3 O Patris caritas!
O Nati lenitas!
Deep were we stainèd
Per nostra crimina;
But thou has for us gainèd
Coelorum gaudia:
O that we were there,
O that we were there!

4 Ubi sunt gaudia, where,
If that they be not there?
There, are angels singing
Nova cantica;
There the bells are ringing
In Regis curia:
O that we were there,
O that we were there!

Little *Jesus* Sweetly *Sleep*

Traditional

Gently and slowly

1 Little Jesus, sweetly sleep,
Do not stir;
We will lend a coat of fur;
We will rock you, rock you, rock you,
We will rock you, rock you, rock you;
See the fur to keep you warm,
Snugly round your tiny form.

2 Mary's little baby, sleep,
Sweetly sleep,
Sleep in comfort, slumber deep;
We will rock you, rock you, rock you,
We will rock you, rock you, rock you;
We will serve you all we can,
Darling, darling little man.

Hark! *The* Herald *Angels* Sing

Music by **Felix Mendelssohn** *Words by* **Charles Wesley**

Moderately fast

G D Em G/D D Bm G C G/D D7 G
Hark! The her - ald an - gels sing___ Glo - ry to the new - born king;

G B Em A7 D/F# G D/A A7 Dsus D
Peace on earth, and mer - cy mild,___ God and sin - ners re - con - ciled.

D G C Em G/D D D G C/B♭ A7 G/D D
Joy - ful, all you na - tions, rise,___ Join the tri - umph of the skies;___

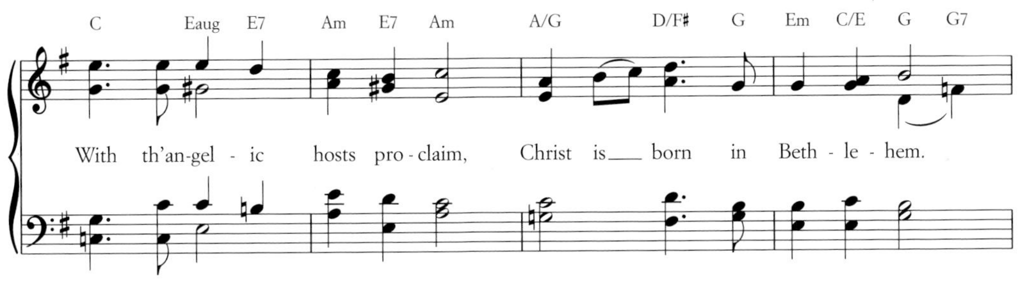

1 Hark! The herald angels sing
Glory to the newborn King;
Peace on earth, and mercy mild,
God and sinners reconciled.
Joyful, all you nations rise,
Join the triumph of the skies;
With th'angelic hosts proclaim,
Christ is born in Bethlehem.

Hark! The herald angels sing,
Glory to the newborn King.

2 Christ, by highest heaven adored,
Christ, the everlasting Lord;
Late in time behold him come,
Offspring of a Virgin's womb.
Veiled in flesh the Godhead see;
Hail, the Incarnate Deity,
Pleased as man with man to dwell,
Jesus, our Emmanuel!
Hark! The herald angels sing . . .

3 Hail the heaven-born Prince of Peace!
Hail the Sun of Righteousness!
Light and life to all he brings,
Risen with healing in his wings.
Mild he lays his glory by,
Born that man no more may die,
Born to raise the sons of earth,
Born to give them second birth.
Hark! The herald angels sing . . .

Deck *The* Hall

Traditional

Brightly

F
Gm
F/C
C7
Deck the hall with boughs of hol - ly,
Fa la la la la, la

F C7 F
F
Gm
F/C
C7
la la la,
'Tis the sea - son to be jol - ly,
Fa la la la la, la

F C7 F
C
F
C
la la la,
Don we now our gay ap - pa - rel,

1 Deck the hall with boughs of holly,
Fa la la la, la la la la,
'Tis the season to be jolly,
Fa la la la, la la la la,
Don we now our gay apparel,
Fa la la, la la la, la la la,
Troll the ancient Yuletide carol,
Fa la la la, la la la la.

2 See the blazing Yule before us,
Fa la la . . .
Strike the harp and join the chorus,
Fa la la . . .
Follow me in merry measure,
Fa la la . . .
While I tell of Yuletide treasure,
Fa la la . . .

3 Fast away the old year passes,
Fa la la . . .
Hail the new, ye lads and lasses,
Fa la la . . .
Sing we joyous all together,
Fa la la . . .
Heedless of the wind and weather.
Fa la la . . .

The Oxen

Thomas Hardy (1840-70)

Christmas Eve, and twelve of the clock,
'Now they are all on their knees,'
An elder said as we sat in a flock
By the embers in hearthside ease.

We pictured the meek mild creatures where
They dwelt in their strawy pen,
Nor did it occur to one of us there,
To doubt they were kneeling then.

So fair a fancy few would weave
In these years! Yet, I feel,
If someone said on Christmas Eve
'Come; see the oxen kneel

'In the lonely barton by yonder coomb
Our childhood used to know,'
I should go with him in the gloom,
Hoping it might be so.

A Christmas Carol

Christina Rossetti (1830-94)

In the bleak mid-winter
Frosty wind made moan,
Earth stood hard as iron,
Water like a stone;
Snow had fallen, snow on snow,
Snow on snow,
In the bleak mid-winter,
Long ago.

Our God, Heaven cannot hold Him
Nor earth sustain;
Heaven and earth shall flee away
When He comes to reign:
In the bleak mid-winter
A stable place sufficed
The Lord God Almighty
Jesus Christ.

Blow, Blow, Thou Winter Wind

William Shakespeare (1564-1616)
from 'As You Like It'

Blow, blow, thou winter wind,
Thou art not so unkind
As man's ingratitude;
Thy tooth is not so keen,
Because thou art not seen,
Although thy breath be rude.

Heigh-ho! sing, heigh-ho! unto the green holly:
Most friendship is feigning, most loving mere folly.
Then heigh-ho! the holly!
This life is most jolly.

Freeze, freeze, thou bitter sky,
That dost not bite so nigh
As benefits forgot:
Though thou the waters warp,
Thy sting is not so sharp
As friend remember'd not

Heigh-ho! sing, heigh-ho! unto the green holly:
Most friendship is feigning, most loving merely folly.
Then heigh-ho! the holly!
This life is most jolly.